MW00416149

Drag-Free Drift

Jeff A. Plemmen
April 2002

Drag-Free Drift

*Leader Design and Presentation Techniques
for Fly Fishing*

Joseph A. Kissane

with LeaderCalc
by Steven B. Schweitzer

STACKPOLE
BOOKS

Copyright © 2001 by Stackpole Books

Published by
STACKPOLE BOOKS
5067 Ritter Road
Mechanicsburg, PA 17055
www.stackpolebooks.com

All rights reserved, including the right to reproduce this book or portions thereof in any form or by any means, electronic or mechanical, including photocopying, recording, or by any information storage and retrieval system, without permission in writing from the publisher. All inquiries should be addressed to Stackpole Books, 5067 Ritter Road, Mechanicsburg, PA 17055.

Printed in the United States

10 9 8 7 6 5 4 3 2 1

First edition

Illustrations by Steven B. Schweitzer

Library of Congress Cataloging-in-Publication Data

Kissane, Joseph A.
    Drag-free drift: leader design and presentation techniques for fly fishing / Joseph A. Kissane; with LeaderCalc by Steven B. Schweitzer.— 1st ed.
    p. cm.
    Includes bibliographical references (p.).
    ISBN 0-8117-0527-7
    1. Leaders (Fishing) 2. Fly fishing—Equipment and supplies. I. Schweitzer, Steven B. II. Title.

SH452.9.L43 K57 2002
799.1'24'0284—dc21

2001042640

For Mary, who tolerates my obsession with fly fishing, and Breanda'n Ruairi', who I hope has inherited it.

CONTENTS

ACKNOWLEDGMENTS

First, a thank-you to Steve Schweitzer for contributing his leader formulas, known as LeaderCalc, as well as his illustrations and general counsel during the final preparations of the text, and to my brother, Mike Kissane, who assisted in the early editing of the text. I also thank Doug Conover, editor of the *Second City Angler,* newsletter of the Elliott Donnelley Chapter (Chicago) of Trout Unlimited, for providing me with a forum for my previous writing in this regard. Some of the information used for this text was gained informally through chance meetings or at seminars, where the individuals were not likely to have known that they would be contributing to this effort. Nevertheless, I wish to specifically acknowledge the following for information or assistance given during the research for this book, intended or otherwise: William C. Black, M.D.; Jeremy Benn (Orvis Company); Gary Borger; Jason Borger; Paul Burgess (Airflo); Bob Guard and Bruce Olson (Umpqua Feather Merchants); George Harvey; Jon Hoffmann; Jon King (J. J. King Fly Fishing); John M. Kissane, M.D.; Lefty Kreh; Jerry Krueger; Clint Pedersen; Dan Pieczonka (Dan's Tackle Shop); Iain Sorrel (Mainstream USA); Don Stazy; Ed Story and Bob Story (National Feathercraft Company); and Dave Whitlock.

INTRODUCTION

The least understood element of a fly fisherman's equipment is the leader. Anglers spend large sums of money on rods, reels, even lines, but place relatively little emphasis on the element of tackle that is second only to the fly in proximity to their quarry: the leader. The tendency to consider an off-the-shelf leader as acceptable is uncharacteristic of the sport of fly fishing. Fly fishermen draw distinctions among tens of thousands of fly patterns; no fewer than twelve different line weights, with dozens of tapers for each weight; and rods that range from relatively inexpensive to luxuriantly handcrafted works of art. Yet many anglers spend less than $5 on a leader and resent that it will not accomplish all the things expected of it. It makes little sense to weaken a wonderfully designed, if not extremely expensive, set of equipment by forcing it to rely on a cheap leader. Conversely, I have seen anglers with inexpensive rods, reels, and waders, but with a basic understanding of the leader and the way a fly drifts, anglers can consistently outfish the guy with the best outfit on the stream.

Just as no single casting style is best for all situations, no single set of rules applies to all leaders. There are a talented few who can perform a variety of casts with a single line and leader, with only minor alterations, but it makes little sense for the rest of us to frustrate ourselves in efforts to make leaders do what they were not designed to do. Once you learn why leaders perform as they do, you will be able to make modifications to accommodate differences in conditions or your casting style. And by understanding the mechanics of how the rod, line, and leader interact, and what factors determine how artificial flies act when you try to make them act like naturals, and then learning which of these factors you have the most control over, you can improve your chances of success.

The purpose of the leader is simple enough: to provide a low-visibility, low-impact transition from the fly line to the fly in such a way that will facilitate a presentation that is appropriate to the type of fly and its intended movement after reaching the water. The leader must be light enough to appear inconspicuous, yet strong enough to hold the fish. And it should allow you to fish the fly in a preferred and controlled manner with respect to drag, drift, and current. There are times when you want the fly to be dragged by the leader, as during a retrieve or wet-fly swing, and there are times when you want to avoid drag altogether, as in most dry-fly presentations. It is unrealistic to expect the same leader to be able to perform optimally in both of these situations; you select the leader that will best suit the circumstances.

A design feature common to most leaders is taper. The taper of a line and leader allows them to turn over in a smooth, controlled manner. In addition to line speed, the factors that control the behavior of a leader are the rate of change in diameter of the material, its stiffness, and its total length. These factors may be used to compensate for one another, as stiffness is a relative function of diameter and length.

There is no right or wrong to leader design, as individuals may be able to achieve the same results with different leaders, depending on the conditions at hand, the level of expertise, and the casting methods used. Leader materials are typically identified by the cross-sectional diameter, in either fractions of an inch or incremental X values, and the manufacturer's breaking strength rating, in pounds. The leader's behavior depends on its cross-sectional area, and its ability to hold a hooked fish depends on its breaking strength. Careful measurements indicate that the manufacturers' listings of diameters are not entirely accurate, however, and the ratings of breaking strengths are conservative. Fly line and leader behavior in the cast also depends on other factors, including the coefficient of friction. Manufacturers have long marketed fly lines and leader materials in general terms of these characteristics, but they do not provide objective or numerical comparisons beyond saying that one line is a certain percentage slicker than another or that one leader material is stiffer or more supple.

This book started out as an attempt to characterize leaders and provide an understanding of them so that readers would feel confident enough to make their own from scratch, first following recipes of others, and then modifying them to fit their style. But as so often happens, the subject of the whys and wherefores of leaders became more than a simple matter. So the whole thing grew, and in the process, I, too, became a student, refreshing old notions and learning new ones. Initially, I was reluctant to introduce technical elements into a discussion of fly fishing, but I eventually came to realize that they were necessary in order to understand the factors that affect leader design and how these factors interact with the drift of the fly.

LeaderCalc came along for the ride as a natural addition to this work. Steve Schweitzer's diligent efforts to compile leader formulas and present them in such a usable form provide the reader with a quick reference and a useful tool for putting the substance of this work to use. An earlier version of LeaderCalc was available free through Steve's generosity, and when he and I discussed this text, we agreed that the two were meant to go together. So a newer version of LeaderCalc, with user documentation and some of Steve's thoughts on leaders, is at the back of the book.

CHAPTER 1

Drag and the Drag-Free Drift

Drag occurs when the flow of water in complex currents pulls the line and leader, causing the fly to travel in response to the movement of the line to which it is tethered, rather than the flow of the water it is directly in contact with. So drag refers to the unnatural movement of a fly in directions different from the path it would travel if it were not attached to a line. Fish can detect drag with great proficiency, and unnatural drift may be the single most common reason for the rejection of a fly.

The nirvana of fly fishing is the drag-free drift. It is something we all must strive for but cannot attain. The laws of physics will not allow it. But still, we try to get as close as possible. So when someone brags of having made a perfect presentation with a resulting drag-free drift, they are exaggerating—or, in other words, practicing what fishermen are best known for.

RECOGNIZING AND REDUCING DRAG

You can take a few moments when you plan a cast to try to minimize drag. Because currents are what cause drag, the fewer current boundaries your line must cross, the less drag will affect it. If possible, stand back some distance and observe the currents, identifying areas where seams and swirls and other complex currents exist. The idea of reading the water has been around for years, yet the emphasis on finding holding water and feeding lanes has obscured the utility of looking at current lanes and opportunities to reduce drag. Unfortunately, with the increased fishing pressure on many streams, stepping back for detailed inspection is often seen as an invitation for other fishermen to move into the area and take a shot. Patience and tact are often required in such situations, and the development of these fine arts is beyond the scope of this work.

If you have the opportunity, look at underwater structures such as logs, boulders, deeper channels, and weed beds, all of which contribute to variation in stream flow. Contrasts in stream flow at boundaries between currents define current lanes. These boundaries contribute to drag. Whenever possible, position yourself for your presentation in such a way as to minimize the number of current boundaries your line must cross. Carefully get closer to your target, or use a longer rod, which will allow you to keep more line off the water. Mending line, or flipping slack loops into it once it is on the water, can help reduce the effects of drag, and longer rods also make mending easier.

Drag can also be caused by vertical turbulence, where water passes over boulders, logs, or other irregularities in the streambed, or as a result of the friction between moving water and the streambed. Vertical turbulence can pull flies downward, exposing them to complex currents and destroying any chances of a dead-drift presentation.

Surface boils and swirls, or "lazy Susans," are often good places to target with searching patterns, but here drag potential may be highest in multiple directions. Both novice fishermen and wise old-timers may seek out such places because large fish exploit "lazy Susans" for their bountiful food supplies, but it is not easy to present a fly here in a manner that acts like a free-drifting food item. Often the best approach in such a situation is to cast a foot or less upstream of such a feature, with plenty of slack in the leader. Then allow the currents to take the fly as they will. As soon as the slack is taken up, gently retrieve the fly and recast. This allows the fly to mimic the natural foods drifting into the vortex of the feature, and equally important, by retrieving the fly and recasting immediately, before severe drag is likely to alert fish to the fact that it is an imitation, you prevent the fish from visually associating your fly pattern with an unnatural drift. Another reason for retrieving the fly immediately is the possibility that it is being mouthed by a fish you have not detected because of the amount of slack in the line; you may have a fish on the line already.

DRAG AND FEEDING HABITS

Why do fish often rise to a dry fly, even leap from the water and come down next to the fly, but seemingly either miss it or flatly refuse it? Having heard many explanations, and having made up numerous excuses myself, I now place most of the blame on drag. It is unlikely that a trout realizes the fly is a fake and consciously refuses it. Trout do not appear put off by seemingly odd variations to natural foods, such as anal hooks or peculiar colors, and they are creatures of habit, pattern behavior, and instinct rather than intellectual preference. A more likely reason for a refusal is that drag intervened between the fish and the fly.

Trout have a keenly perceptive sense of motion that allows them to combine visual observation with influences of detected vibration and an almost gyroscopic sense of balance. All of these factors go into the timing of a fish's rise to a fly. The rise or jump is timed based on the fish's perception of the surrounding current and its own location with respect to the drift of the fly. Once the trout commits to the rise or jump, because of the speed and acceleration involved, it is difficult to change directions. If the fly is moving contrary to the predicted path, the fish cannot help but miss it. Drag from a leader and fly line is not natural, and the trout does not have the intellect or experience to figure out how to compensate. The trout rises or leaps to where the fly should be, based on its perception of the way the fly should drift. Often the difference between this and the actual drift is so close that the trout appears to miss or refuse the fly at the last instant. This is almost certainly the case when a trout becomes airborne and "refuses" a fly.

A fish cannot see food as it goes into its mouth. As a trout nears the fly, it has to rely on the expected drift and its own movement to catch the fly in its mouth. If the fly is at the water's surface, there is a greater potential for visual distortion. Glare, ripples, and surface debris all are factors that impede the trout from catching a fly on the surface. If a trout pulls its head from the water or leaps to catch the fly, its vision is further distorted by the sudden change from water to air. If, in addition to all of this, drag enters into the equation, the chances of connection are further diminished.

But what about subsurface feeding? If a trout is relying on its perception of drift, how can it catch a moving larva imitated by a nymph or a minnow imitated by a streamer? And what about dapped or twitched dry flies or terrestrials on the surface? It seems that trout have multiple modes of feeding and pursuit. A dead-drifting fly is sensed as a food item at the mercy of the current, but for patterns that are fished with some implied or induced movement, be they wet flies, streamers, nymphs, or terrestrials, the trout must rely on active attacks. This requires a different mode of feeding, and a trout is not very good at switching between feeding modes quickly, let alone in midpursuit. That is why if you watch a trout feed, it usually feeds in the same way for a prolonged duration. When foods like relatively placid mayflies are drifting to the trout, it is energy-efficient to plan the interception of drifting foods, rise to them, and indulge, with a minimum of effort. If the food is more active, say caddis or hoppers, the trout must operate in a different feeding mode or wait for a meal that better suits its program.

In *Caddisflies,* Gary LaFontaine reported the results of research that showed, in general, that trout tended to feed in patterns with little or no opportunistic deviations. He stated that it took over one thousand encounters with a previously unknown food item before a trout would routinely take or imprint on a particular fly. Based on this, you should forget about notions of "creating a hatch" with some pattern that you decided to try out of the blue. If it works, it is probably just luck, or you may have accidentally mimicked the behavior of something the trout was used to seeing. But this observation is also important in considering that drag cannot readily be input into a trout's response to a fly.

The change or transition in feeding programs may be responsible for the phenomenon observed when a prolific hatch occurs but is seemingly ignored by the trout in the area for the first several minutes, or even several daily cycles of the hatch. Some have observed that the trout are usually taking the subsurface emergers that precede the adult stage of the fly, and that is probably true; however, it is also likely that the trout are in the mode of feeding on subsurface emergers and are not as capable (for the most part) of switching programs back and forth from subsurface to surface feeding. Once the emergers are diminished and the trout are keyed on surface patterns, they may be as unlikely to go back to subsurface patterns until the supply of adults declines.

Some fishermen believe that fish that become airborne are often propelled out of the water by the acceleration they must use to collect caddis pupae rapidly rising through the water column. The observation that they sometimes come crashing down on a surface fly as they return to the water is presumed to be fortuitous. This implies a level of deftness that is difficult to attribute to even the most admired of fishes. And it goes against the notion that opportunistic feeding is not entirely common. Is it possible for the trout to plot a course to intercept one food item in ascension, then gymnastically adjust the reentry into water to pounce upon another food item?

All of this conjecture seems to be trashed by the 20-inch brown trout caught on a Yellow Humpy or a hopper, or even a #18 Adams, and found to have a small crayfish in his throat, yet to be fully swallowed. That is, until we consider how this guy got so big. First, he got so big by avoiding predators like himself or us for a few years while he grew up. He avoided predators by being smarter than the average fish. And he also got so big by being capable of switching back and forth from one mode of feeding to another. Is he the norm? If he were, we would not see pictures of people proudly holding 12-inch brown trout in spring creek settings. They would all be 18- or 24-inch predators. He is the exception; he is smarter or more adaptable than his fellows, but he was not smarter than the fisherman, or we never would have heard the story.

MINIMIZING DRAG WITH S CURVES

George Harvey, regarded as one of the great experts on leaders and drag, has experimented with leader design for over fifty years, using a variety of materials. In an effort to learn the relative importance of drag and leader diameter, he duplicated earlier experiments using live insects threaded with short segments of leader materials and allowing them to drift freely in the current over feeding fish. Harvey found no significant difference between the number of free-floating bugs taken with no leader material and those with even relatively large-diameter segments of leader material attached, provided their drift was unaffected. This experiment led to the notion that fish are more discouraged from taking a fly by its being dragged in an unnatural fashion than by the presence of a line attached to it. He discovered that slack in the leader in the form of S curves significantly reduced the impact of drag. The end results of his research are leaders that will induce a series of S curves, as the ultimate goal of the leader, rather than acting simply to transfer energy to get the fly as far from the line as possible. Toward this end, Harvey limits the use of very stiff materials in his leaders. A leader that is too stiff will not respond to small and complex currents. It will drag, and when the leader drags, the fly must drag with it.

Thus one of the best ways to minimize drag is to present the fly on a supple leader that falls in a series of S curves on the water. The leader material should be flexible enough to bend with the crosscurrents in the water. The combination of suppleness and S curves allows the fly to move more in response to the water that surrounds it than the pull of the line. In conjunction with this, you can further reduce drag by planning an approach that minimizes the number of current lanes your line and leader will cross.

The formation of S curves aids in fighting drag by supplying slack line that can be taken up with minimal resistance by the drifting fly. When a fly pulls on a straightened leader and line, it must overcome the friction between the entire "tight" section and the water surface, and the current cannot pull the fly enough to move the whole length of line and leader without drag occurring. S curves provide slack so that only the length of the first half of the S resists the free flow of the fly; the other half of the S curve is actually in sync with the current and lets the fly drift relatively unencumbered.

As the drift proceeds, the line tends to lose these S curves and slack, and drag becomes an increasing problem. What usually happens, though you may not always see it, is that the S curves straighten out in sequence, starting with those closest to the fly, and progressing toward you. What happens in the leader with respect to the S curves may or may not be different from what happens to the line, depending on the design of the leader and the results of the cast. A well-designed and well-cast leader will hold S curves even as the line starts to straighten. This is because the leader's surface area and mass are so much less than those of the line that it is less susceptible to the various currents. If, however, you follow conventional wisdom and make a perfect transition between the leader and line, in terms of energy transfer and mass, it is likely that the S curves in the total system will straighten out from the fly down the leader to the line. When this happens, it is possible, even likely, that by the time the S curves in the line start to straighten out, the leader may have already straightened, and drag will have begun to alter the natural drift of the fly. And effectively mending the line and leader is very difficult, especially with longer casts.

To achieve the longest natural drift, it is best that the S curves in the line-leader system not straighten out entirely sequentially. You can prevent this by interrupting the smooth energy transfer from the cast through the line to the leader, manifested as the loop in your cast, at some point before the end of the leader. Various leader designs can help in this regard, as discussed in later chapters.

The more slack, the less drag; the more S curves, the more slack. The size of S curves can be important with regard to the width of the current lanes that the line crosses. For a starting point, to be effective, the wavelength—the length of a complete S curve—should be, at most, half the width of the current lane it straddles. If it is shorter, there will be even more slack, and this is better, up to a point.

If the current lane is so small that it is impractical to cast S curves that are smaller than the width of the lane, you might consider approaching from an oblique direction, which will lengthen the distance across the lane,

An ideal cast incorporates a series of curves in the line to aid in fighting drag. In this case, the riffle has a series of current lanes of varying speeds, and the line crosses them in a series of S curves.

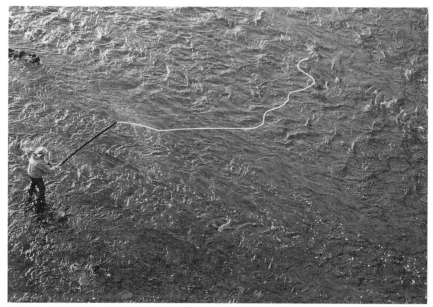

After a short time, the line starts to straighten out and is pulled into a downstream belly.

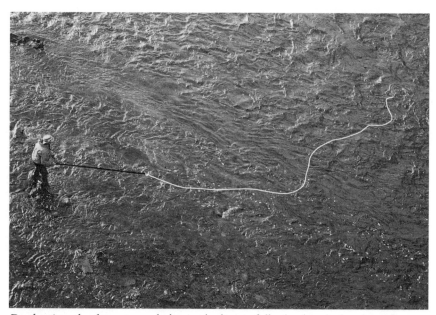

By the time the downstream bulge in the line is fully developed, drag has taken control of the fly.

allowing you to use longer S curves. Another option is to cast from a position that is directly in the lane, eliminating boundaries altogether. Still a third option is to cast gently, but close to the target, so the visible drift of the fly is brief and the fish has less time to detect drag.

The size and number of S curves are determined by the combination of leader design, casting mechanics, line weight, and the aerodynamics and hydraulics at the time and place where the cast is made. The interplay of all of these factors is far from simple. Among the important factors of leader design that affect the formation of S curves are the number and type of knots used, as each knot is a potential flex point or node in the curve.

Understanding what causes the formation of S curves is helpful, as these S curves are a very desirable feature of leader performance, especially when using smaller flies, as in most trout fishing. A combination of factors contributes to their formation. By understanding these factors and controlling them, you can further control the drift of the fly and reduce the effects of drag.

The simplest reason for the appearance of S curves in the leader might be that the segments of leader material are not straightened or have not been joined in a straight line due to the type of connection (knot or loop) used, and consequently, the leader is not straight when at rest. But straightening a leader before use is necessary to prevent tangling of the line and to facilitate controlling its behavior in the cast, so this factor may be minimized. Other causes include the wind and the action of the leader during the final instants of the cast. The type of cast plays a critical role in whether the leader will tend to straighten. If you accelerate the rod at the last instant and the line straightens out immediately before it hits the water, S curves will be minimized. Conversely, if this acceleration occurs an instant earlier, the leader will straighten out in midair and then recoil with an intensity proportional to the degree of acceleration, resulting in S curves—or a tangled mess if the cast is severely overpowered at the end. If, on the other hand, the cast is underpowered at the end, desirable slack may be generated because of incomplete turnover. This phenomenon likely occurs at least as often unintentionally or accidentally as deliberately, with many fish caught by fishermen hastily retrieving what they believe to be poor casts.

Another, more complicated, explanation for the formation of S curves lies in the physics of the loop and the line in the cast. An understanding of the basic behavior of a wave may help explain the formation of S curves in a leader. As the energy of the cast moves down the line, manifested by the loop, as the crest of a wave, it ideally will move smoothly through the air, as there are only minor changes or contrasts in the line to cause it to break up or dissipate. When the energy wave hits a boundary, such as the union of

Lengthening tippet by adding 2 or 3 feet will automatically add S curves to your leader on present action because there is so much tippet that it can't fully straighten out.

the line and leader, part of it is reflected backward a small distance, and part moves forward. The part that moves backward forms small S curves in the line behind the leader butt section. The energy wave moving forward is refracted at an angle different from that of the original loop, at a different speed, causing the wave to decay, and this creates S curves in the first segment of the leader. This process continues as the energy wave encounters each knot in the leader, forming a series of S curves. Thus the knots themselves are responsible for the formation of S curves because they are not perfectly linear and induce reflection and refraction in the energy wave, whereas the knotless tapered leaders available on the market will not form S curves with nearly the ease of a knotted leader. This can be demonstrated by comparing the behavior of leaders made by splicing identical segments of line with leaders that consist of a single piece of line of the same diameter, or by cutting and retying a knotless leader and comparing the number and size of S curves that result from casting it before and after the operation.

I don't think this is sensible— even to consider hardly.

You can adjust the length of the segments of a leader to increase or decrease the size and number of S curves. The absence of S curves altogether may result in so much drag that the fish is alerted to the unnatural conditions and stops feeding. If the cast does not turn over, collapsing prematurely, you can correct the problem by altering the design of the leader or applying greater energy to the cast. If a cast does collapse, the leader is still likely to allow a reasonable drift because of all the slack in it, so you should allow the fly to run its course before recasting. If you try to immediately collect the slack from a poor cast, the awkward swirling of the line is more likely to alarm the fish than if you allow it to straighten out on its own. Again, many fish have been caught by accident in such situations.

ASSESSING CURRENT LANES

Reducing the effects of drag on the drift of your fly is easier after you have determined the locations of current lanes in the stream. Currents of contrasting velocities will pull the line and leader at different rates than the fly itself, inducing drag.

Once you have assessed the stretch of water and identified obvious lanes of contrasting current, you should try to determine whether smaller, more subtle lanes exist within the larger currents. There are a couple ways to accomplish this. First try to determine whether the water within a short distance, say 30 feet, is likely to hold fish. It is usually best to begin by working the water closest to you, then work your way out to more distant water. If you see a fish rising farther out and wish to pursue it first, that is your choice, but you may spook closer fish in casting and positioning yourself to go after the more distant target. The fish you alarm may flee toward

Always inspect and consider fishing the water closest to you. The downed tree and boulders here will direct deep currents and also provide cover for fish.

your target and alarm the fish you are after. Unless the more distant target is rising to a very short-lived hatch, it is not likely to stop feeding in the time it takes to prospect the closer water.

You can gain some very real benefits by first working the water closest to you and gradually increasing your casting length. You will obtain an understanding of the surrounding stream currents by watching the line drift after each cast. Cast with only the leader outside the tip-top of the rod and observe the drift of the fly and line within 10 or 15 feet of you. This will allow you to assess the leader's adequacy in terms of length and minimal drag. Strip off 10 feet of line and cast farther. Observe the curves that form in the line as it drifts to see where the surface currents are moving fastest and slowest. If you cast straight upstream, only one current lane should affect the line.

As you lengthen your casts, the apparent contrast between these currents may seem to decrease because the line does not appear to move at different speeds between you and the target. This means that drag is already acting on your line to a greater extent. Having made this determination, you can add more slack line to the cast by inducing more and bigger S curves with an abrupt stop at the end of the cast. You can also modify the drift by mending the line once it is on the water.

Surface bumps indicate submerged boulders that result in a number of intersecting current lanes both at and below the surface.

If you are fortunate, you may encounter a fish or two in this process. Maybe one will come along that is big enough to make you forget about that riseform 50 feet upstream. If not, you have still gained a better understanding of the dynamics of the stream, and these are what determine the best approach to take to minimize drag when pursuing a distant target.

Current speed varies as water flows around obstacles like boulders. Water is incompressible, so waves form when currents of contrasting speed and direction collide or when water collides with an object in its path. Water flowing directly into the upstream side of a boulder in midstream will be slowed by the collision and spread around the obstacle, and water flowing alongside the boulder will be squeezed in its path by the deflected water. The water in current lanes near the boulder or one of the banks will be slowed by friction from these side constraints. Current lanes that slide alongside the boulder coalesce on its downstream side. If the stream is flowing with enough volume or gradient, this will result in a turbulent vortex. Otherwise, the currents will slide around the boulder, coming together in a slow eddy or pocket of water with almost no downstream component. The result is a complex situation of slow water immediately upstream of the boulder, with current lanes increasing in speed toward the middle of the path between the boulder and the bank.

In the case of a single large boulder in the middle of the stream, two areas of little or no downstream flow are produced: one upstream and one downstream. The upstream low-flow pocket is a crescent-shaped wedge where the water sometimes bulges upward. This is a prime target area for large fish, as it is the first (upstream) low-flow holding water where a fish can wait for food. Because trout are competitive, the largest ones are often found here. The other pocket of low-flow water is the triangular wedge behind the boulder where the currents coalesce. This is also a prime spot for trout, as food often swirls in the small crosscurrents.

The diagrams show the currents in the case of one boulder. The situation is more complicated when there are many boulders of various sizes. Here the currents are superimposed on one another, deflecting each other and causing more slack-water areas than there might be with individual independent boulders. This is called pocket water, because pockets of slack water are scattered throughout.

Once you have identified the major and possibly minor currents between you and the distant fish, think about whether your leader is properly configured to deal with these currents. If not, make adjustments before your next cast, or you may spook the fish and never get a second chance. Next, determine the best approach. Count the number of major and

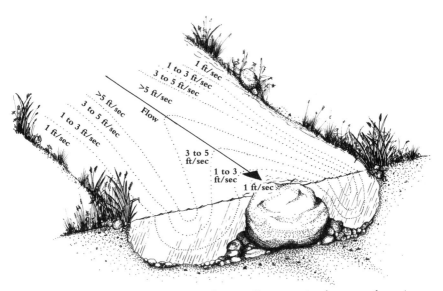

The case of a single large boulder in midstream illustrates simple current lanes in two dimensions and current tubes in cross section. In this case, the slowest current is found along the banks and immediately upstream of the boulder, and the fastest current is found approximately midway between the bank and the boulder.

minor current lanes that lie between you and the fish. Try to design your approach—your position and the direction from which you will cast—so that your line and leader cross the fewest possible current lane boundaries. Each of these boundaries represents a potential source of drag, and minimizing the number of lanes crossed is critical to reducing overall drag. This is the reason for the success of classic upstream dry-fly presentation—it minimizes drag by reducing the number of current lanes to one. If you can quietly move a few feet in one direction or another and thereby reduce the number of lanes your line will cross, do so. When wading, move your feet carefully to minimize vibration and disturbance of the streambed and the current.

Once your cast is made, follow the drift carefully. The old advice of following your fly with the rod is really only half true. If your leader is well designed, the fly will drift fairly well so long as you properly cast the line with adequate S curves to accommodate contrasting current lanes. You should follow the end of the line, rather than the fly, with the tip of the rod. To prevent the line from pulling against the fly, keep the rod tip lower at the upstream end of the drift, slowly raising it as the fly passes your position, then lowering it again as the fly drifts downstream. This will keep the fly in the same current lane in a relatively straight path. Extending your arm a foot more during the drift may enable you to eliminate one or more lane interfaces that your line will drift across. As the line drifts, you can assess the effects of drag by watching the S curves changing shape. Seeing the S curves start to straighten is a warning sign that drag is occurring or that you have a fish on the line.

You may add to the length of the drift by feeding out additional line as the fly drifts downstream, but it is best to do so before the line starts to drag. Once the S curves in the line start to straighten, drag has already occurred. Any remedies used after drag has started are less likely to be successful in continuing a dead drift, because the leader has probably become too straight to absorb the effects of more drag. This is not to say that you should abort the drift at this stage and recast. Traditional wet-fly tactics rely on the transition from dead drift to the arcing tail of the drift, often with fish hitting the fly as it begins to drag. Wet flies are usually being fished in the near-surface film of the stream by this time, even though they are wet flies. The real distinction between a wet fly and a dry fly is often no more than the traditional direction of the initial cast—upstream versus downstream. Always fish out the whole drift.

VERTICAL DRAG

The last article Lee Wulff published was a brief discussion of using colored ribbons on a wading staff to allow you to detect and visualize crosscurrents.

In my study of drag and all of its various contributing elements, I found that there is some merit to this method. Its major drawbacks are that it essentially requires that the stretch of water be wadable and that you not care if you spook every fish within eyesight of the wading staff or that anyone watching may think you a bit odd. Wulff may have acknowledged the second drawback by conceding that the observations are best made long before you plan to fish or after you and anyone else in the area are finished fishing this stretch of stream for a while.

The velocity distribution in a straight stretch of smooth-bottomed stream depends on the slope, depth, and width of the channel. The fastest current is at the center of the channel, immediately below the surface. This is because of the slowing effects of friction on the bottom and sides, and the effects of wind drag on the surface at the middle of the channel. But nature does not provide smooth-bottomed channels, nor would we be as attracted to streams if they were so monotonous. Every rock and fallen tree acts to divert currents, and the result is the beautiful environment we enter to pursue trout.

The apparent calm of the surface of the North Platte River here is not indicative of the complex currents at depth. Using polarized sunglasses, you can identify boulders that alter the current and plan your approach and cast accordingly. You can also trace bubbles on the surface to identify subtle surface currents.

The observations gained by watching the staff ribbons would allow you to determine the extent to which nature's nonuniformity has altered the currents from the ideal and show what kind of vertical velocity profile exists in the stream at different stations. Once you have found contrasting currents in the vertical profile, you may wish to interpolate the current velocities upstream and downstream from the observation stations, so long as the basic streambed shape is essentially similar. Knowing this, you could plan the type of subsurface approach you wish to use—what kind of weighting, if any, would be necessary for your fly to reach the depth at which the fish are holding and the length of leader to use. By combining the observations of surface lanes from casts and the vertical profiling from the staff and ribbon method, you can form a mental three-dimensional conceptual model of the various current "tubes" in the stream. Once you have the three-dimensional model in your head, you can imagine a subsurface fly tethered to a line by a leader and plan your presentation accordingly.

Beginning fly fishers often become obsessed with trying to read the stream to locate fish. Once anglers have located fish, or water assumed to hold fish, they often tend to be eager to get a fly to a feeding fish, without giving enough thought to how that fish will perceive the presentation. Even the most realistic imitation of a natural trout food will fail to induce a strike if poorly presented. Conversely, trout will strike an object that bears only the slightest resemblance to a food item if it is properly drifted within their feeding zone.

Trout do not survive to become large by exposing themselves to risk. Such fish may be wary of an object that resists the natural drift of the stream, but they often deem an object that is drifting along with the current worth more than a second look. A trout often lets a fly drift past it to observe it from several angles before giving chase and striking. It is that second look that we strive for, and the strike is the reward for our patient efforts.

FLIES AND DRAG

The kind of fly used also makes a difference regarding drag. Flies that are required to float high on the water are normally hackled. In general, the more rapid or turbulent the water, the bushier the hackle needs to be, as this will cause the fly to ride higher on the water's surface. Thus less of its mass comes in direct contact with the surface, and as a result, such flies may be more susceptible to the drag of the line than to the flow of the water on which they are floating. The inertia of the line and leader may cause them to be held back as the water beneath them moves on, and this is drag. This is something to consider when selecting flies. Patterns with the hackles on the underside clipped have become the trend on some waters. Such a pattern may be more successful because the fly is more likely to follow the currents of the water around it than if it could ride on the hackle tips when dragged by the line or leader.

Another aspect of hackles is their impact in the subsurface. Woolly Buggers and similar patterns are highly susceptible to currents because of their hydraulic resistance to flowing water. This means that they will be pulled around by currents more so than more streamlined patterns. These patterns also tend to twist as they drag, whether during a drift or a stripped retrieval. This twisting is transferred to the tippet and leader as a whole and can permanently impart twists or curls into the leader. When using such patterns, it is important to use a stiffer or more durable tippet material to compensate for this twisting. The same twisting occurs when casting bushy flies, wet or dry, as the wind catches the hackles and twists the fly at the end of the tippet. The paradox of this is that bushy flies are used in the West on bigger rivers, where the winds are also more prone to cause twisting and casting problems. So the bushier flies that are preferred because of the "bigger" water are contraindicated by the windy conditions that prevail there.

The twisting of subsurface patterns like large nymphs or streamers also results in an unnatural appearance to the trout. Many patterns are designed as though they drift naturally, like the Bitch Creek nymph, with a light-colored underside and a dark-colored back. When the fly is dragged and twists on the end of the tippet, the light-colored underside cannot possibly appear natural to a fish, as no natural nymph is capable of the kind of pirouetting movement that results. The Brooks Stonefly nymph and a number of other similar patterns are tied in the round so that they appear the same regardless of the side from which they are viewed, reducing the "barber pole" effect of twisting underwater flies.

There is no easy solution, and as with many challenges, you have to be aware of the potential problem so you can adjust either your leader or flies accordingly. A weighted fly is less likely to spiral during a dead drift than it is on a tight line, so you can minimize this effect by fishing the fly on a dead drift more than a stripped retrieve. A stiffer leader will resist twisting better than a fine, flexible tippet. Subsurface conditions may allow you to use heavier materials, and you should consider adjusting your tippet accordingly. A weight placed a short distance from the fly will act as an anchor and will limit the twisting to the distance between the fly and the weight, except where the current is very strong.

Make frequent inspection of the leader a part of your routine, especially with weighted flies. Countless times, I have watched people unknowingly cast snarled or twisted leaders that have no chance of catching a fish because the fly was wrapped up in the tippet.

CHAPTER 2

Leader Dynamics

To understand leader dynamics, it helps to have some background on the material properties of rods, lines, and leaders. Let's begin by comparing the characteristics of importance in a rod, a line, and a leader in order to see the transition that occurs.

Aside from weight, the physical characteristic with the greatest effect on casting and on line behavior during a cast is flexibility. A material's diameter and modulus of elasticity, the extent to which it will deform in response to stress, are what largely determine its overall flexibility or stiffness. The greater a material's diameter, the stiffer it will be. A tree trunk, for example, is stiffer at its base, where it is thickest, than near the thinner top. This relationship between thickness and flexibility is a primary controlling factor in the design of lines and leaders.

For a fly rod, the most important physical property is the modulus of elasticity. When you make a cast, applying energy through the hinging of the elbow, the rod flexes. When the cast is complete and the energy is no longer being applied, the rod recovers to its original shape. The second most important consideration in a rod is its mass, as an angler may make several hundred casts a day. The mass also determines the degree to which a rod will flex or load during a cast. The rod's inertial resistance (a consequence of the rod's mass) to the movement imparted by the caster helps load the rod, so weight is a double-edged sword. We need it to load the rod, but too much of it will add to our labor and make casting less of a joy. Because of the leverage of a rod, the importance of mass increases from the butt to the tip. An extra few grams of weight are insignificant in the butt section but may have profound impact on the tip section. The third most important characteristic in a rod is its cross-sectional geometry, as this relates to its flexibility. The designers determine the casting character of rods by adjusting the wall thickness and varying the diameter from butt to tip in the rod's taper. The wall thickness and diameter determine the rod's weight and stiffness. These physical properties of a rod are thus interrelated and determine all of its other major characteristics. Other important considerations, based on the types of water you will fish, are line weight and rod length.

For a fly line, the most important physical property is its weight, as this is a determining factor in how much the rod will flex when the weight acts to resist the rotational acceleration imposed by the caster's elbow. The weight is also a factor in the line's ability to float or sink. The weight of a line is so fundamental to its behavior that this is the basis of line classification, and rods are designated by line weight as well. The second most important characteristic of a line is the geometry of the taper. Taper determines weight distribution to some extent, as well as flexibility. The third most important factor in a line's behavior is its flexibility. A line that is cast is not necessarily going to end up in the same shape as it was before the cast, so the flexibility of line is a viscoelastic, or plastic, property. The fourth characteristic is the line's coefficient of friction, which determines how well it will slide through the guides of a rod as it is cast. There are also secondary considerations, including the line's diameter, as this affects its wind resistance.

For a leader, the properties of primary importance are flexibility, weight (as a component of density), friction, and possibly color. Like line, a leader can behave viscoelastically, so these properties are similar. But weight, which is essential in loading the rod for the cast, should generally be minimized in a leader, as too heavy a leader will straighten out too severely and create a wake when it hits the water. Though stiffness is desirable in rods, fly lines, and to some extent in the energy-transfer segments of leaders, it is generally undesirable in the presentation segments. Friction, on the other hand, which is undesirable in a line, becomes an asset in leaders, as tying knots with slick materials is a serious problem.

Material Properties of Rods, Lines, and Leaders

Property	Rod	Line	Leader Section Energy Transfer	Presentation
Stiffness	Desirable	Varies	Desirable	Undesirable
Weight	Undesirable	Desirable	Undesirable	Undesirable
Diameter	Important	Moderately important	Moderately important	Important
Color	Unimportant	Moderately	Moderately	Important
Friction	Unimportant	Highly undesirable	Desirable	Desirable

Though the fundamental assumptions and principles developed by the early pioneers of leader design were not based on the physical properties of modern materials, their applications continue today. The giants of leader design in the past, Charles Ritz and even George Harvey, for a good part of his career, lived in the era of cane, silk, and gut. Rods were generally heavier and more flexible. Silk lines also were heavier and more flexible than modern lines, and industry standardization may not have been as precise as the current standards. Gut leaders tended to be more supple than modern leaders of nylon and fluorocarbon, and the fact that gut was not man-made limited the length of strands available. The traditional design principles were based on interactions between lines and leaders, in terms of transfer of energy and flexibility, that are significantly different from those used now, unless one is fishing with a traditional set of equipment. The casting styles used with more flexible rods are quite different ("slower") from the casts made with high-tech graphite rods and synthetic lines and leaders. Whereas silk and gut were pretty close to each other in terms of weight and flexibility, the physical properties of modern fly lines with plastic coatings are generally much different from those of the typical monofilament leaders. It is essential to keep this in mind when applying the principles of past experts.

COMPARING LEADER MATERIALS

In order to intelligently modify or improve leaders when conditions change or you wish to try something different, it helps to understand the nature of leader materials and be able to compare them consistently. Most of the important properties of leader materials are dependent on the type of material and its diameter. The most common modern leader materials today are nylon and fluorocarbon, and a number of other blends and polymers, such as polyurethane and polyethylene, are now coming into play as the manufacturers start to explore the market. The properties of these materials that are most important to drag are modulus of elasticity and specific gravity, or the density of the material compared with that of water. It is these properties that determine material stiffness.

Another property of leader material worth considering is the refractive index, a comparison of the velocity of light passing through the material with that of light passing through a vacuum. This is important, as it determines the degree of light scatter, or glare, generated when light passes from one material to another, such as between air, leader material, and water. The greater the difference between the refractive indexes, the more light will be bounced off as glare, so a material that has an index close to that of water will be less conspicuous, because it will not produce as much glare.

This assumes the surface is not scratched or textured in a way that would alter the optical properties.

Physical Properties of Leader Materials

Material	Specific Gravity	Modulus of Elasticity, psi	Refractive Index
Water	1	not applicable	1.33
Nylon	1.05 to 1.25	700,000 to 1,250,000	1.5 to 1.65
Fluorocarbon	1.65 to 1.95	75,000 to 200,000	1.4 to 1.45
Polyurethane	0.75 to 1.5 (highly variable)	25,000 to >100,000 (highly variable)	(highly variable)

Definitions:

Specific Gravity: Density of the material divided by the density of pure water (unitless)

Modulus of Elasticity: Standardized measurement of Stress divided by Strain (pounds/square inch)

Refractive Index: Ratio of the speed of light passing through the material divided by the speed of light in a vacuum

The slickness of a leader material also plays a role in its suitability. Slickness is defined by a material's coefficient of friction. Fluorocarbon is considerably slicker than nylon, as it has the ability to diminish friction between surfaces. This is a factor in knot tying; for example, if you use three wraps for a blood knot on a 3x or 4x nylon leader, you might need four wraps on a fluorocarbon leader of the same diameter.

The characteristic that is most important in the way a leader behaves during casting and the drift is stiffness, as determined by modulus of elasticity and specific gravity. Though weight is a factor in the performance of a fly line, the major concern with the weight of a leader is whether it will float. And with the exception of specialty rapid-sinking leaders, the significance of whether a leader floats is secondary. First, it has to perform properly in the cast and when it lands on the water.

Leader recipes are traditionally written with reference only to the diameter of the material, which has a direct effect on stiffness, durability, and strength. European recipes are typically given in terms of the breaking strength (BS) rating. Breaking strength is typically expressed in pound-test, which is more variable than diameter in terms of how accurately manufacturers are likely to report it. The influx of new manufacturing and material technology into fishing lines has complicated this matter by making it possible to have materials that are identical in diameter but different in terms of stiffness, strength, abrasion resistance, color, and even refractive properties, which affect how readily fish will see the leader. So it is no longer enough to specify only the length and diameter of each segment in a leader recipe. To be complete, a leader recipe should include the length, size, and manufacturer of each segment, as well as the knot or type of connection used for each union. Once you become familiar with the relative stiffness of various manufacturers' products, it then becomes important to note where the leader uses stiff versus more supple materials. Problems may still arise if a manufacturer changes the properties of materials or discontinues a product.

As part of his comprehensive treatment of fly-fishing equipment, John Merwin, in *The New American Trout Fishing,* presents a wish list of things he would like to know about leader materials or leaders. The list includes the line and fly size for which leaders are intended, accurate leader length, accurate diameter, accurate strength, age, elasticity, knot strength, flexibility, abrasion resistance, and color. To this list, we might add whether the leader will float, and whether the finish is matte or glossy. Packages providing all of this information might have to be significantly larger than they are now, or we might have to read fine print that would make us yearn for something as easy as tying a #20 midge. But Merwin's point is that we are usually not given nearly enough information.

LEADER STIFFNESS

To accurately describe leader stiffness, the single most important factor in determining the way a leader behaves when cast or during the drift, it was necessary to develop a numerical index that can be understood easily and described in terms that most fishermen can either visualize or actually conduct their own tests to verify.

After attempting to get information from manufacturers and receiving constructive responses from only a few, I conducted a review of the engineering properties of flexible materials. The degree to which a line will bend can be derived mathematically if a set of variables is known.

Nylon, the primary material used in leaders, is a relatively well-defined polymer with limits to the variability of its properties. Plasticizers may be added to the nylon to vary its flexibility within a range, but this has less influence on performance than the diameter, which is the most important factor in the flexibility. From the study of elastic materials, the degree to which a cylindrical beam—the technical description for a nylon line with a circular cross section—will deflect or bend is determined by the following formula:

$$\text{Deflection} = \frac{4 \times L^3 \times F}{3 \times \pi \times E \times r^4}$$

where: L = the length of the line extending from a support point such as the tip of the rod

F = force, the downward force applied by gravity

π = 3.14

E = modulus of elasticity of the material

r = the radius of the leader material in cross section

It is true that leaders and lines do not behave as purely elastic bodies. They behave transitionally between elastic, where the volume of the body remains essentially the same as deformation occurs, and viscoelastic, or plastic, where the volume changes during deformation. It is this difference that makes it physically impossible to achieve a continuously gradual transition in energy transfer from the rod, which behaves purely elastically, to the leader. But without delving much deeper into the world of engineering and material sciences, we can still use the elastic deformation as a simplifying illustration.

The actual force applied to the cylindrical beam is determined by the weight, which varies according to the taper and length, and the dynamics of the cast, all considered in the determination of what is called the moment of inertia. The derivation of the moment of inertia is more complex than the simple multiplication of the formula above and would be extremely complex for a simply cast line, let alone one that includes shooting line. The point of this discussion would not be served by further derivation, because the diameter clearly dominates the equation, by virtue of its exponent of 4. The length of the material has an exponent of 3, which makes it a very important factor as well, but in comparing one material to another for this example, the length will remain the same.

So the stiffness of any elastic cylindrical body is proportional to its cross-sectional radius raised to the fourth power. Doubling the diameter multiplies the stiffness by 16 (2 to the fourth power). For example, keeping all of the material properties above the same, let's compare a 0.004-inch diameter (7x) material to a 0.008-inch (3x) material (0.002-inch and 0.004-inch radius, respectively). Using the equation, we raise 0.002 to the fourth power (= 0.000000000016), and compare it with 0.004 raised to the fourth power (= 0.000000000256). So the factor in the equation for radius is sixteen times greater for 3x material compared with 7x. And because r^4 is in the denominator, deflection will be sixteen times less for the 3x material, i.e., 3x is sixteen times stiffer than 7x, all other considerations being equal.

Regardless of whether the leader behaves elastically or plastically, length is also an important factor, having an exponent of 3. Doubling the length of a segment has the effect of increasing the deflection by $(2)^3$; that is, it will bend eight times as easily. Therefore, you can compensate for a material's stiffness by lengthening the segment if you wish to maintain the same strength or flexibility. In practice, we do this all the time. Longer tippets are designed for this very purpose. If we kept segment lengths the same all the way down to the tippet, we would not get the best presentation and degree of slack.

As previously mentioned, the other major factors that determine leader stiffness are the material's modulus of elasticity (E) and specific gravity, or density (which determines the force acting to flex the material). And because nylon is a material with a relatively limited range of physical properties, the value for E will not vary greatly.

Deflection Vs. Line Diameter

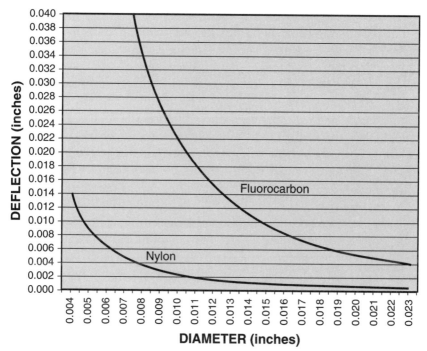

Plot showing the relationship between deflection under gravity and the diameters of nylon and fluorocarbon leader materials.

The effects of using other materials in leaders can be determined by comparing the values of E for some alternatives. The derivation of E is based on the amount of strain resulting from a measured stress. The relationship is a simple division:

E = stress ÷ strain

stress = the amount of force applied to the product

strain = the amount of deformation, be it stretching or compression

strain = final minus initial dimension ÷ initial dimension

The present range of graphite composites used in fly rods is in the neighborhood of 33 million to 66 million pounds per square inch (psi). Nylon monofilament lines tend to have a modulus in the range of 700,000 to 1,250,000 million psi, making them about thirty to fifty times less stiff than the average graphite fly rod, without considering the diameter of each. Polyurethane plastics tend to have values of E in the range of from 30,000 to 100,000 psi, and fluorocarbon and Teflon materials tend to be in the range from 75,000 to 200,000 psi.

The relationship between diameter and relative stiffness is shown in the graph above, with reference to available monofilament sizes. The graph is a plot showing the deflection of a 1-inch segment of line under its own weight and how the degree of deflection, as an indication of line stiffness, is decreased as line diameter increases. The lines represent the most common materials used in leaders—nylon and fluorocarbon. To construct the graph, the length and the modulus of elasticity for each type of material are held at the same constant value and only the diameter of the leader changes. This also changes the value for the load, as the weight of the leader increases with diameter.

Specific gravity, weight, and mass are terms that have standard definitions in physics and engineering but are mistakenly used interchangeably by many in describing the property that is commonly known as weight. Specific gravity has the most relevance to the subject at hand. Materials that have specific gravity values greater than 1.0 will sink in water, because they are more dense ("heavier") than water. Materials with specific gravity values less than that of water will float, as they are less dense than water. There is a difference between flotation and buoyancy. A material with a specific gravity greater than water may float as a result of surface tension, as a steel needle can be floated on a glass of water. If pressed down under the water, it will stay below the surface and sink. A buoyant material is less dense than water and will float even after being submerged. Line and leader dressings can aid in flotation by increasing surface tension and actually increasing the effective diameter of the leader by adding a film around the surface of the material that has a certain thickness. The net result is a composite of leader and dressing with a total specific gravity less than that of water, so it floats and is buoyant.

Fluorocarbon line typically has a specific gravity of 1.65 to nearly 2.0 and consequently is used for leaders drifted below the water surface. Nylon typically has a specific gravity in the range from 1.05 to 1.25, so if used undressed, it tends to sink slowly, unless the surface tension supports it. Polyurethane has a wide range of specific gravity values, which can be as low as 0.75, and may be suited for applications where flotation and buoyancy are desired.

Consider the equation for deflection, which shows how important diameter is, and the range of diameters of leader materials commonly available. Then, considering the range of values for E of various materials used for leaders, from 30,000 to 1,750,000 psi, it is possible to achieve a great degree of variability of stiffness when constructing leaders.

MANUALLY COMPARING LEADER STIFFNESS

By making two small loops of the same diameter with two materials, and pushing each in with a finger, you can qualitatively tell which is the stiffer material by the amount of resistance to the push. This can be accomplished using the simplest of tools: a ruler and your fingers. You can use a pencil or similar small object if you are uncertain of the objectivity of your finger. Rest the pencil on the tight loops and compare the deformation of each.

Two materials can also be compared side by side in their response to moving air. Straighten equal lengths of two materials, about $1\frac{1}{2}$ inches, and then hold them together by one end between your thumb and forefinger. Then blow on the dangling ends and observe the two materials bending. A stiffer material will resist bending more than one that is less stiff.

You can make relative measurements of the stiffness of various materials, substitute like materials for each other, and expect them to perform similarly. By evaluating the stiffness of tippet materials, you may be able to substitute a stronger tippet that will behave similarly in cases where you believe you will need greater strength, without sacrificing the properties of the leader design. This also means that if you exhaust your supply of a favorite tippet material, or the manufacturer discontinues it, you may quickly find a reasonable substitute by testing materials that are available.

You can check a material's flexibility by using the loop test.

By systematically evaluating the factors in leader performance, and understanding what controls these factors, you should better be able to prepare leaders designed for specific uses based on the experiences of others, determine why particular leaders do or do not perform well, and readily adjust the various components in a leader to improve its performance in response to changing conditions or if you want to change your presentation.

CHAPTER 3

Rods, Lines, and Rod Flex

All of the physical components of fly fishing should be selected to interact cohesively. It is no more appropriate to try to gently present a #22 midge with a 10-foot, 8-weight rod than it is to hunt rabbits with an elephant gun. But not everyone can afford a collection of different fly rods matched to every situation one is likely to encounter, so anglers often have to make do with what they have.

FLY RODS AND LINE WEIGHTS

Fly rods are sized by line weights. Line weights are standardized by the American Fishing Tackle Manufacturers' Association (AFTMA), as determined by general standards adopted by the manufacturers in 1961. The standard line weights are based on the weight per foot, in grains, of the front 30 feet of line, as this was presumed to be the most common amount of line cast by the average fisherman. Though a 30-foot cast may have been average in the early 1960s, today 45 feet is closer to the norm with the higher-modulus graphite rods, so this standard may be out-of-date.

AFTMA Standard Fly Line Weights
(based on first 30 feet of line)

	Line Weight (grains)		Actual Weight (ounces)	
	max	min	max	min
0★	54	58	0.123	0.133
1	54	66	0.123	0.151
2	74	86	0.169	0.197
3	94	106	0.215	0.242
4	114	126	0.261	0.288
5	134	146	0.306	0.334
6	152	168	0.347	0.384
7	177	193	0.405	0.441
8	202	218	0.462	0.498
9	230	250	0.526	0.571
10	270	290	0.617	0.663
11	318	342	0.727	0.782
12	368	392	0.841	0.896
13★	435	465	0.994	1.063
14★	485	515	1.109	1.177
15★	535	565	1.223	1.291

★not yet standardized
Source: *The Technology of Fly Rods,* Don Phillips, 1999.

Standardized line weights for fly lines assigned by the American Fishing Tackle Manufacturers' Association (AFTMA). Note that there are gaps between line sizes that allow some flexibility in designation of lines not within one range or the next.

As Darrel Martin, in *Micropatterns,* points out, line weights do not overlap, so lines whose weights fall between two designations are legitimately entitled to be either or both. An appendix to *Micropatterns* includes detailed graphs of the weight distribution of various fly lines. One can use these to predict how one line will compare with another in casting and loop formation.

In the interest of allowing different manufacturers to maintain some degree of uniqueness, the weight distribution and diameters of the various lines are not standardized. And different manufacturers use materials that may be closely guarded secrets to achieve special line characteristics such as stiffness, buoyancy, or slickness. This permits designers to play with the diameters and buoyancy (diameter determines volume and thereby affects specific gravity if weight is kept constant). There is also no formal standard as to what constitutes a weight-forward or double-taper line. But the fly-fishing community is steeped in tradition and convention, so there is a tendency for industry to coin new terms for lines that fall outside of the "conventional" weight-forward and double-taper types, such as "triangle taper" and a host of others, rather than stretch the definition of standard terms beyond the norms. The standard nomenclature of fly lines also includes a designation as to whether the line floats, sinks slowly, or sinks more rapidly in quiet water. The letter designation F (floating line), I (intermediate sinking line), or S (sinking line) is added to the AFTMA line code, so that, for example, a DT3F is a double-taper 3-weight line that floats, and a WF7S is a weight-forward 7-weight line that sinks. So the system provides a reasonable means of comparing lines with one another.

For most presentations where drag and precision are considerations, a floating line is preferred because it is easier to control and to see on the surface of the water than below it. If you cannot see the line, it becomes difficult to assess the effects of drag, even with one or more floats on the leader and line. Additionally, floating lines facilitate mending because it is easier to pick up a line off the water surface, and to do so with less disturbance, than a line that has descended into the water column and must be pulled upward before breaking the surface.

There are certain applications where a sinking line or a line with a sinking tip is preferable. Fishing deeper-water flies in deep stillwater may be best accomplished with a sinking or sinking-tip line, depending on the type of movement you wish to impart to the fly. A weighted line will result in movement during the retrieve that is consistent with a creature moving parallel to the bottom of the stream or lake, whereas a floating line will impart movement that has a significant vertical component, such as the movement of a creature that rises and descends as it drifts or moves.

ROD LENGTH

Rod length is also an important consideration, because it affects the length of cast you can easily attain; however, rod weight, both in terms of the line weight and actual weight of the rod, affects the comfort and ease of casting, which are probably more important considerations when selecting a rod. All of these factors are interrelated. It is generally good to use as long a rod as you can comfortably manage, as the longer the rod, the less effort you have to exert to cast, and the more readily you can mend line once the cast is made. The rod is a lever, and the longer the lever, the easier your work is. A longer rod also allows you to keep more line off the water, so it is less susceptible to drag. Nevertheless, smaller rods still have their charm and character, and few of us would give ours up willingly.

ASSIGNING LINE WEIGHTS TO RODS

There is no established set of standards for assigning line weights to rods. The manufacturers are fairly consistent about calling one type of rod action a 5-weight versus a 7-weight. And the fly-fishing publications are diligent in reporting deviations from convention in this regard. However, you may be surprised by the level of performance of rods marketed for a particular line weight when cast with a line one size over or under (referred to as overlining or underlining).

Rod manufacturers tend to design rods with line weights for circumstances anglers are most likely to encounter, both in casting and managing a fish once hooked. Thus you are not likely to see a 12-foot, 5-ounce rod for a 2-weight line, or a 7-foot, 2½-ounce rod for an 8-weight line. The same 30-foot logic that is applied to line weights is also applied to rods, so a 5-weight rod is designed to easily lift 30 feet of 5-weight line and maintain tight loops in casting with that line. Modern graphite rods allow manufacturers to stretch this 30-foot criterion to as much as 45 feet in most cases. The rods are designed to impart the degree of flexure desired by the manufacturer under the load of the line in casting, which tends to become a signature of the particular design of rod, so that one rod manufacturer becomes known for a certain type of rod action. The subtleties or stark contrasts between different models allow you to tailor a rod to your casting and fishing styles.

Rods are designed for the circumstances you are most likely to encounter, both in casting and fighting a fish. A 2-weight rod is not designed to handle a 25-pound salmon, and in the lighter weights, the properties of a rod that make it a pleasure to cast take precedence over its ability to land a large fish. On the other side of the spectrum, rods manufactured for larger fish are designed so that fish-fighting takes priority over casting ease, because it would be useless to hook a 25-pound tuna with a beautifully executed cast, and then not be able to land it.

A method of determining the best line weight to use with a rod, whether or not it is marked by the manufacturer, is to determine the extent of flexure, or loading, that occurs in response to both the weight of the line and the casting motion. Casting motion is specific to each individual and is not readily quantified. So it may be best to use a correlation based on the rod's stiffness in response to weight. Jon Hoffmann of California Polytechnic State University, Matthew Hooper of Northrup Grumman Corporation, and Al Kyte of the University of California–Berkeley have come up with a scheme based on this. In spite of the intimidating credentials of the authors, their calibration test is simple enough for the average fisherman to perform.

A clamp, a ruler, and a small scale are all the equipment required. Assume the rod flex length (L) to be the total length of the rod in centimeters, minus the handle. Clamp the rod handle in a horizontal position, and suspend a small weight from the tip. Measure the deflection, in centimeters, of the tip from the unweighted horizontal position to the weighted position, and designate this distance as "D." The ratio of the weight in grams divided by D is referred to as "stiffness." The calibration is considered valid if the deflection from horizontal is less than 10 percent of L. The rod stiffness is considered to be the ratio of weight per unit of deflection, so long as the deflection is less than 10 percent of the rod's flexible length. This value will be somewhere in the range of .25 to 3 grams per centimeter of deflection.

Hoffmann, Hooper, and Kyte plotted the stiffness calibration for twenty-two fly rods compared with the AFTMA line ratings for each rod. The line weight values were based on line-to-rod matching by an experienced casting instructor, Al Kyte, rather than on manufacturers' designations. In cases where rods performed well with more than one line weight, Kyte assigned weights between the AFTMA whole numbers. For example, a rod that cast well with a 4 or 5 weight but performed better with the 4 weight, received a line rating of 4.25. The manufacturers' ratings are added to the plot to show that there is room for differences of opinion on which line is best for which rod.

The authors of the study then plotted a "best fit" line through the test data points (ignoring the manufacturers' points) and added a shaded area to show the range of line weights that will likely work best with various stiffnesses. For example, a rod that flexes 5 centimeters with a 5-gram weight has a stiffness of 1. The curve on the graph shows that a stiffness of 1 corresponds to a 6- or 7-weight rod. This calibration method should be considered a guide, not an inflexible rule.

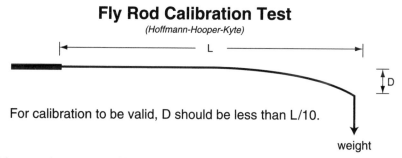

Fly Rod Calibration Test
(Hoffmann-Hooper-Kyte)

For calibration to be valid, D should be less than L/10.

weight

Schematic depicting variables used in equations for rod calibration.

Fly Rod Calibration Plot

(Hoffmann, Hooper, and Kyte)

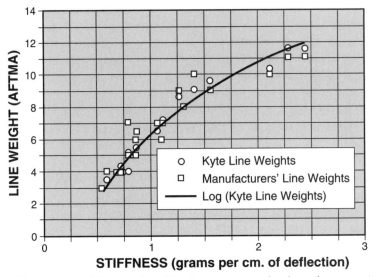

Plot of data for fly-rod line weight calibration. Incremental rod weights are assigned based on closeness to the next line weight. For example, a 5-weight rod that is close to a 6-weight in performance is assigned a weight of 5.75.

Hoffmann, Hooper, and Kyte recommend using the graph to help match lines to rods whenever you are in doubt as to what line you should use to cast most efficiently. This method allows recalibration of repaired rods, homemade rods, or rods that may vary from the manufacturers' designations because of modifications or variations in placement and weight of guide wraps. It also permits a relatively simple way to compare rods.

STIFF VERSUS SOFT ACTION

Inconsistency often occurs when considering the action of a fly rod. Terms such as *fast, slow, stiff,* and *soft* are thrown around without hard definitions as to what these terms imply. Rods behave differently with respect to loading during casting. During the cast, there is a level of flexure at which the rod most effectively stores potential energy. The greater the load on the rod, the more energy is stored. The optimum flexure occurs where the stored potential energy is rapidly released in the forward cast. If the energy is released slowly, the cycle of the cast must be timed at a slower rate and may become laborious. When the rod is not adequately loaded, either because the timing in the cast or the weight of the line is insufficient to provide enough inertia, potential energy is stored, but not enough to efficiently assist the cast. The act of casting is not likely to allow flexure beyond the failure point, especially with higher-strength composition rods.

Although there is a specific rod blank design called *progressive,* the flexing of a rod during loading is progressive by its very nature, regardless of the design. The tip flexes first because it is thinnest and closest to that which loads it—the inertia of the line. As the tip is flexed further, it reaches a load sufficient to cause bending progressively deeper in the rod, toward the handle. The amount of flexure necessary to load the middle and butt sections of the rod determines whether the rod is considered fast, medium, or slow.

Soft-, slow-, or wet-action rods are generally those that show bending, or loading, beyond the halfway point of the rod under normal casts of 30 to 40 feet. Slow-action rods flex well into the thicker portion of the rod long before the tip section is flexed to its greatest potential. The term *soft* originates from the physical description of the material as relatively soft acting. The term *slow* refers to the slow recovery in oscillation and flexure. These rods have a low natural frequency. The time required in the casting stroke for a slow rod to reach its optimum loading is longer than it is for a stiffer, or fast, rod, and casting strokes will be slower as a result. *Wet* action refers to rods better suited for wet-fly fishing, in the strictly traditional sense. Other slang terms, such as "noodles rods," are also used to describe extreme cases of slower rods. All of these terms are essentially synonymous.

Fast or stiff rods are stiffer than their counterparts. These rods normally exhibit flexure only in the upper half during a normal cast. They tend to have faster recovery from flexure and oscillation, and require a faster casting stroke. The term *fast* refers to the action of a fly rod that when oscillated, or wiggled, returns to a resting position relatively quickly. These rods are characterized by a higher natural frequency. These rods load rapidly, reaching their optimum load with less effort than a slow rod. Because these rods are preferred to cast dry flies and keep them "dry" as a consequence of higher line speed, they are also referred to as having dry-fly action. All of these terms are essentially synonymous.

These terms hark back to the days of cane (bamboo) or even greenheart (wood) rods. With advances in rod taper design in the 1970s and 1980s, tapers that varied the flexibility of a rod at different points along it were developed, and terms like *simple* and *progressive* taper were coined as carryovers from the engineering professions. Simple tapers tend to be tapered so the blank gets thinner at a constant rate or the bending in the rod progresses downward at some constant rate. There is no formal definition.

Progressive tapers have been developed that increase in stiffness from the tip toward the handle to a greater extent than does a simple taper. This is primarily accomplished by altering the diameter along the rod's length in such a way that the longitudinal cross section is concave, although some manufacturers use graphite of different stiffnesses in different sections of multipiece rods to achieve the same result. Rods with progressive tapers often have more flexible tip sections than rods with simple tapers; this is an advantage in casting short distances or where more delicate presentations are necessary, adding a level of versatility to the more complex rods.

Rods are more rigid than fly lines, so their behavior with respect to flexibility can be accurately described by elastic analysis. The stiffness is accurately described by the equation used earlier to describe the behavior of a solid beam:

$$\text{Deflection} = \frac{4 \times L^3 \times F}{3 \times \pi \times E \times r^4}$$

where: L = the length of the rod extending from a support point such as the edge of a table

F = force, the downward force applied by gravity,

$\pi = 3.14$

E = modulus of elasticity of the material (the engineering property that describes the degree to which a material will deform (strain) in response to stress)

r = the radius of the rod blank in cross section

There is a craft to rod manufacturing that, although quite different in the design of graphite rods compared with cane rods, can result in rods of greatly varying character constructed from the same material. Cane rods have a unique character imparted by nature into their material, because each bamboo strip contains a variable number of natural fibers, each with potential variability. The craftsman making a cane rod evaluates these qualities, assembling the rod in such a way that they complement each other. Fiberglass rod manufacturing diminished the uniqueness of each rod, but fabrication inconsistencies resulted in rods of the same make and model having a range of variability and action. Graphite rods are made of modern materials and are manufactured under very close tolerances, using technology that has advanced significantly in the past twenty years. They are, therefore, far more consistent in character than either cane or fiberglass, but there remains some variability.

A "more is better" mentality has developed in response to increasingly high-modulus graphite rods. But the equation above shows that a rod with a modulus of elasticity of 33 million psi can be made as stiff as one with a modulus of elasticity of 54 million psi simply by increasing its radius or wall thickness. This alters the rod's mass somewhat—by fractions of an ounce—which can affect performance and feel when applied over the entire length of the rod. There are very fine 33 million psi graphite rods and very mediocre 54 million psi graphite rods. Nevertheless, even a mediocre graphite rod will outperform the best fiberglass rods of twenty-five years ago, with the advantage of significantly lighter weight. Comparing cane rods with graphite, on the other hand, is like comparing Babe Ruth with Mark McGwire: The behavior characteristics and the circumstances make comparisons difficult.

There may be less than fifty makers of graphite rod blanks in the United States, but there are far more rod makers selling their wares, and both generic and name-brand rods are available. There also are do-it-yourselfers who prefer to custom-make their own rods from rod blanks. Rod-making companies and individuals alike can alter the performance of identical graphite blanks by altering other components of the overall rod design.

The above equation shows that radius, modulus, and weight all have a bearing on the way a rod will bend. Weight can have a significant effect on the amount of deflection of a graphite rod, as it is such a lightweight material. Because the rod acts as a lever, the action of weight is multiplied by the distance from the effective fulcrum—the place where the casting hand holds the handle—of the rod. Intuitively, it makes sense that a small weight has little effect close to the handle but will result in larger deflections as it is moved outward toward the tip of the rod. This explains several behavioral traits in fly rods. Shorter rods tend to be stiffer, unless they are thinner as well. Longer rods will load deeper—bend farther during the backcast—throughout the length of the rod than will shorter rods with otherwise similar design.

The effect of weight on a rod's action can be used to alter the rod's character in design and manufacture in more subtle ways. If you decide to build your own rod, you may discover that the seemingly insignificant weight of individual guides and the thread wraps that hold them in place change the way the rod flexes when you wobble it in your hand. When you coat the guide wraps with lacquer or epoxy, the effect becomes even more noticeable. You can alter the number, placement, and length of thread wrap to fine-tune the flexibility characteristics of a rod. The thickness of the seal coating used on the wraps may also alter the rod's character.

Several manufacturers now offer rods with single-foot rod guides, designed to effectively cut the weight of wraps in half and thereby retain more of the original rigidity of the rod blank. These guides offer some advantage in this regard, but this benefit is gained at the expense of long-term durability.

If you build a rod yourself, you may feel inclined to test the rod blank's action as you would a finished rod by wiggling it while holding the butt section. The action of the blank will, however, be significantly slowed by the addition of guides and tip. You can see how much difference the weight of guides makes on the action of a rod blank by tightly wrapping rubber bands on the blank at the locations of each guide, and then wiggling the blank as you would a rod. Using masking tape may provide a better simulation, but you may not want to try this with a blank you do not own. If you base your selection of a blank on the performance of a finished rod and want to have the same action, try to replicate the guide placement and wrapping to the greatest extent possible. If you prefer a softer feel or a slower action, you can modify the action in this direction by lengthening the wraps, using a thicker coating of sealer on the wraps, or even tightening the spacing of the guides to add one more. You can stiffen the action by reducing the size of wraps, but most manufacturers are at the minimum level anyway, so your only alternatives may be to go with single-foot guides or widen the spacing and eliminate one guide, which is not always recommended. As a last resort, if you want to be really precise, you can grind the feet of the guides down to a smaller length, thereby shortening the necessary wrap lengths, and reducing the amount of sealer as well. Most snake guides are built on a machine that winds the wire around a rod, and the length of the feet is not based on strength as much as it might be on the size of the guide. Just be careful not to shorten the feet so much that you jeopardize the strength of the guide.

The "more is better" mentality has become a "faster is better" trend as well. Faster rods tend to be better suited for distance casting, as they are stiffer and consequently load more energy into the cast. The emphasis on ever-lengthening casts comes at a strange time in American fly fishing, as the crowding of larger, more prominent waters is driving more and more fishermen to explore remote spring creeks and smaller water in general. It seems odd that we would want rods designed to cast 75 feet to pursue trout in streams small enough to jump over. Shorter casts require less energy, and the ability to impart subtle variation into the cast may be better accomplished with more delicate, softer or slower rods. It was not so long ago that fly fishermen used rods we would scoff at as "noodle soft," and did so quite effectively. The fastest cane rods were slow compared with the stiffer fiberglass rods of the sixties and seventies, and graphite composites keep getting stiffer and stiffer.

THE ORVIS FLEX INDEX

Although efforts to quantify stiffness in leaders have not been definitive, the stiffness of rods is another matter. The parameters involved in rod stiffness are simpler because the rod behaves entirely elastically, with no viscoelastic complication. The flexibility of a rod varies as one goes down the taper, and this characteristic is used by rod designers to produce rods with unique performance traits. Orvis currently markets its graphite rods using a flexibility index system that takes this into account and measures rod flexibility with respect to length. Other manufacturers may use their own methods of characterizing rod stiffness and taper, including diagrams and graphic comparisons of rod deflection under loading.

To assign an index to a rod, Orvis developed a method of bracing the rod at 45 degrees so that it is supported at the handle, approximating where the caster's hand acts as a fulcrum. The rod is then loaded with a weight that is based in some degree on the fly line of the appropriate weight. The loading weights are also assigned in such a way that the rod is not over-loaded, so the flexure is limited to the upper half of the rod.

To measure the flexibility, the rod is clamped in place and the weight is suspended from the tip. A set of measurements is made of the geometry that results. After determining the point at which the rod's flexure begins, the rod length is divided into two segments: a straight portion and a curved (flexed) portion. The length of the straight line section is A and the curved length is B. The flex index is computed by the following equation:

$$\text{flex index} = [(A/B) - 1] \times 10$$

Orvis Flex Index

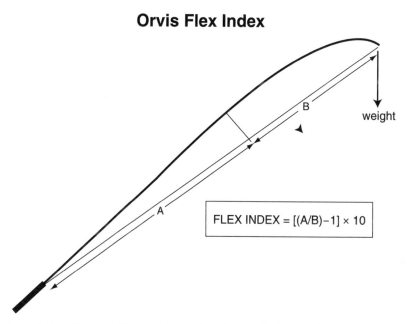

FLEX INDEX = [(A/B)−1] × 10

Schematic depicting variables used in Orvis rod flex calculations (from Orvis technical representative Jeremy Benn).

Orvis Rod Flex Index
Test Weights by Line Weight

Line Weight (AFTMA)	Test Weight (oz.)
1	2.2
2	2.73
3	3.26
4	3.79
5	4.32
6	4.85
7	5.52
8	6.19
9	6.86
10	7.93
11	9.82
12	10.63

Table of test weights used in assigning the Orvis rating to rods (data from Orvis technical representative Jeremy Benn).

By limiting flexure to the top half of the rod, the value is always positive; if flexure extended beyond the halfway point, the ratio of A/B would be less than 1, and the flex index would be negative. The higher the flex index, the stiffer the rod. This system has many merits, not the least of which is that it can be used by anyone with a minimum of equipment and mathematical analysis. It can help you purchase a rod of similar characteristics if a rod breaks or if you wish to obtain similar rods in other line weights. The ratio of A/B allows you to determine the depth to which the rod will flex under the load of the line, which determines, in large part, the action of the rod—the deeper a rod loads, the slower it will tend to be.

Another possible use of the index is to determine how the same rod will perform with respect to various line weights. There are no police out there in the woods to prevent you from fishing a 3-weight line on a slow 5-weight rod if you want it to behave more like a fast-action rod or if you want to lessen the impact of the line on the water. Nor will many people notice if you use a 6-weight line on a 4-weight rod to help load the rod when casting into a stiff wind or to increase your distance.

THE PHILLIPS STIFFNESS PROFILE
Another method was first reported by Don Phillips in a 1973 article in *Fly Fisherman* and subsequently in his book, *The Technology of Fly Rods* (1999).

Phillips experimented with synthetic materials, including fiberglass, boron, and graphite, as replacements for cane from the 1960s through the 1980s. He used his experience as both a materials engineer and an innovative fly-rod designer to come up with a system to characterize rod stiffness. Using the basic engineering properties described earlier, wherein E = modulus of elasticity and I = the moment of inertia, he designed a test device to measure flexure of various segments of the rod under load, computing stiffness as follows:

$$\text{stiffness (EI)} = (\text{load weight} \times \text{length}^3) \div (3 \times \text{deflection})$$

The stiffness of the rod was measured in 1-foot increments and the results plotted on semilog paper. The resulting curves showed the response of the rod to weight throughout the length. The Phillips method is more descriptive than either the Hoffmann-Hooper-Kyte or the Orvis method, as it tests individual sections of the rod independently, resulting in a "fingerprint" curve unique to the rod, which can be compared with that of other rods. The closer the curves are in both shape and actual stiffness values, the more similar their action. Phillips developed the method using cane rods, which by virtue of the natural materials in them and the handcrafting of each rod have a tendency to be very individualistic. The method was developed in the pregraphite era, probably as a means of comparing rods that tended to vary considerably even within make and model. Today's graphite rods are far more consistent in their performance than even fiberglass rods, but there is still some variability.

Fly-rod makers are not likely to resort to the rigid type of indexing that exists with respect to fly lines, as the demand is not there. As long as the public continues to buy rods described in subjective and general terms, industry will be slow to change. It is one of its many paradoxes that fly fishing, although not static, is slow to accept some new notions, yet it welcomes other innovations or fragments of modern engineering or science, such as the introduction of graphite and advances in the studies of entomology.

COMBINING ROD CHARACTERISTIC TEST METHODS

The Hoffmann-Hooper-Kyte method for matching rods to line weights in terms of overall stiffness and the Orvis rod flex test both use similar methods. The data from stressing a rod with a load can then be used both to evaluate the appropriate line weight (Hoffmann-Hooper-Kyte) and to provide a rating of whether a rod has fast, medium, or slow action.

The rod must be properly braced so that only the portion from the forward end of the handle to the tip is free to bend. Then you apply a series of loads using weights from the Orvis test weight table, measuring A and B for each of the weights, as well as the vertical deflections. Although it is assumed that a single "best" line weight exists for the rod, the reality may be that the rod will fit the Hoffmann-Hooper-Kyte curve at several line weights. By applying the Orvis test, using A and B, however, you can assess the relative action of the rod at various line weights, and you may even decide that you prefer its action with one line weight over another, based on these tests. If you have lines of various weights, you can conduct final field trials using each, but you may instead want to use the test results to decide which lines to buy to best meet your preferences.

All of this assumes that the weights used for the Orvis test are appropriate to the Hoffmann-Hooper-Kyte method. If flexure from weights in the Orvis table are more than 10 percent of the flexible length, the line weight may be approximated by assuming a degree of what engineers call "creep." Creep is the reason that the line weight to flexibility plot is not a straight line. The response of a rigid material to increasing stress is that the stiffness, measured by the modulus of elasticity, increases slightly with the load. This is the reason behind the 10 percent limit in the Hoffmann-Hooper-Kyte method. Knowing this, you can interpret results from tests where the deflections exceed 10 percent by matching the rod to a line weight one less than might otherwise be derived from the curve.

SELECTING THE ROD FOR YOUR STYLE

What rod should you buy? That is not an easy question to answer, nor is there a single answer. It is also unlikely that you will take all of the testing and evaluation into account when you select a rod. It is more important that you select a rod you are comfortable with than one that is the most expensive or has the highest-strength graphite. The type of rod you buy should be based on the type of fishing you will do with it. Your casting style should also play a role. Some casters switch styles depending on the rod they use; others try to apply a single style to rods of varying lengths and stiffness, only to find that they cannot achieve the same level of performance with all rods.

A stiffer rod usually is better suited to longer casts, heavier lines, and a faster casting style. In spite of advertising hype, line speed is under the control of the caster, not the rod, just as automobile speed is presumably under the control of the driver. If, however, you choose to cast a softer rod with a higher line speed, your loops will cross or you will wind up cracking your line like a bullwhip. And if you try to cast a stiffer rod slowly, you will find that it is underloaded and requires more effort to cast than it would by trying to match the line speed to the design of the rod. These generalizations are not universal, however, nor do they apply to specialized rods like Spey rods. Unless you are willing to adjust your style to the rod or believe that you do not really have a single casting style, and may develop one to suit the rod, you should avoid buying a rod you have not cast.

Longer rods provide the greater leverage necessary to cast longer lines and heavier flies and to fight strong wind. Stiffer rods tend to handle the additional weight of more line and heavier flies. Softer rods are preferable where fine tippets and small flies are fished on glassy smooth water, as they provide a wide range of control over line speed and make it easier to perform gentle presentations by virtue of lighter line. Softer rods also load more easily with lighter line, allowing soft, slower presentations at closer range. So, for example, if you characterize your style as fast or dry-fly, or if you plan to cast greater distances, you may want to lean toward a longer, stiffer, 5- to 7-weight rod. If you are likely to fish more often where wind is not much of a factor or on smaller waters, you may prefer a 4- or 5-weight rod. If you cast heavy flies or fish where wind is a great factor, you should consider a longer, stiffer, 6- or 7-weight rod. If you tend to fish shorter distances, with lighter tippets and smaller flies, a medium-action, 8- to 9-foot rod, for a 4- to 6-weight line may be best.

Shorter rods, less than 8 feet long, are used for convenience and in tight spaces. Longer travel rods—three-, four-, or even five-piece—are now available that are better than the two-piece rods of ten years ago, but when you are scurrying through the brush, you may find a shorter rod to be advantageous. Beyond the brush, however, they have no advantages over longer rods. Longer rods not only provide greater leverage for casting, but they are better for drag reduction on two counts: Every foot of rod is a foot of line that need not be in contact with drag-inducing water. And the leverage that is useful in casting makes mending that much easier too.

Beginners may be caught up in the fast-line hype and want to go with the newest and stiffest graphite creation on the market. Faster rods allow beginners to cast greater distances; however, without knowing the effects of all the crosscurrents in the water between them and their fly, the distance can be as much a disadvantage as an advantage. Beginning fly fishermen should be encouraged to perfect presentation skills on casts of 30 to 50 feet before trying to launch their flies to new distance records. Faster rods also require faster arm movements that, without adequate control, can lead to more tangles in the lines and leaders of a beginning caster. Medium-action rods, in contrast, allow you to observe the line during the cast and provide a better feel for the moment when the backcast should end and the forward cast should begin. All of this is not to say that the medium-action rod is the tool of the novice. Many experienced fishermen prefer medium-action rods for their delicate presentation. It is safe to say that more than two-thirds of all trout caught on flies are caught within 40 feet of the fly fisherman, so the necessity of a superfast high-modulus rod can be questioned for anyone at any skill level.

Progressive-taper rods, designed with softer tip action and stiffer butt sections, load easily at short distances with low line speeds but have enough stiffness to provide power for longer casts or windier conditions. Progressive-taper rods that are well designed can fill a variety of niches and perform well in each set of circumstances. The softer tip sections protect finer tippets, while the stiffer mid and butt sections are sufficient for bigger fish or more rigorous conditions.

Fast rods do have their places. Wind, bigger streams and lakes, and heavier or larger, more wind resistant flies are all best combated with a faster rod. Once you have become attached to a stiffer rod and learned its loading points and how to manage its qualities, you can achieve delicacy when needed. A fast rod with high line speed can also be an asset in producing S curves in your presentation. Timely interruption in the forward cast with a high line speed will cause the line to fall with beautiful S curves. And certain techniques, like skipping a small dry fly on the surface of the water, are easiest when using a fast rod. But these things take more time to learn and can also be done with medium-action or progressive-taper rods. Besides, if you want instant gratification, fly fishing may not be your best choice as a pastime.

CHAPTER 4

Leader Elements

Energy is what moves fly line, and the efficient transfer of that energy from the rod to the line in the course of the cast is critical. Tapered lines and leaders are more effective in transferring energy through the cast because they use thicker, heavier, and stiffer line to move, or turn over, thinner, lighter, and more flexible line. This helps maintain line speed and makes casting easier. The rules of conservation of momentum and energy apply to the loop moving from the line to the leader.

Momentum is the product of mass and velocity, so a loop of heavy line moving slowly may impart a greater velocity to a lighter line or the leader. Extreme cases of this may be visualized by thinking of how a slow-moving bowling ball might cause a beach ball to jump on contact, or how slowly—if at all—a bowling ball might be moved by a beach ball hurled against it. In a tapered line, the momentum of the heavier line is carried through the loop to the finer line, and the speed of the loop increases because if momentum remains constant and mass decreases, velocity increases. Some leaders are designed to use momentum to turn over the leader more so than the transfer of stored potential energy in a stiff leader. These leaders use heavier, softer materials, and the line momentum is carried down the line in the course of the forward cast, turning the leader over in a tight, high-speed loop.

In the course of the loop's travel in the cast, some momentum and energy are lost as a consequence of external friction in the form of wind resistance and internal friction required to bend the fly line and leader as the loop moves from the end of the rod tip to the fly. The loop also slows as the line uses energy to resist gravity as it stays in the air above the water. The casting arm may actually slow the line as well, by dampening momentum during the cast. If the speed of the cast is to be maintained, or only gradually slowed at the end of the cast, some aspect of the line and leader must compensate for the loss of energy. The taper of a fly line and leader is designed with this in mind. The transition from a fly line that weighs several times what the average leader material weighs enables the loop speed to be maintained, by conservation of momentum, at least enough to prevent loop collapse at the connection between the two materials, even if a relatively inefficient connection is used.

In addition to momentum, the energy from the cast is transferred from the energy of movement, or mechanical energy of the motion, to potential energy stored as the rod and line are flexed, and then back to mechanical energy as the rod and line unbend. Stiffer lines or leaders turn over more readily, all other things being equal, because they perform more elastically than softer leaders, and the transfer of energy from potential to mechanical energy is more efficient.

TURNING OVER

The term *turning over* describes the final opening of the casting loop of a well-designed and well-cast leader matched to an appropriate fly. As the loop of the cast moves toward the end of the line, the fly line and the fly turn over from a position facing the direction of the cast to a position facing the caster. If the leader is unable to turn over, the cast prematurely terminates in the collapse of the loop and possibly results in a tangled mess. The ability to transmit enough energy to turn over a fly depends in large part on the weight and aerodynamic characteristics of the fly involved, so a well-designed leader must be matched to the type of fly used.

Good leaders are often referred to as being stiff enough to turn over easily. This implies that the material is stiff enough that the leader loops are not as prone to collapse or cross over themselves. A stiffer material, up to a point, is easier to control than a limp line that will not support smooth loops, especially if any wind is involved. But relatively limp leaders can turn over well if the weight is properly distributed to maintain enough momentum for the loop to flip over.

Leaders used years ago were made of much limper materials, and turning over was more a function of their mass and the momentum of the cast moving the loop. Nylon changed the nature of the leader in this regard. Years of evaluation of and debate over the appropriate stiffness of the butt section and adjustments in casting techniques coincided with changes in fly rods from cane to fiberglass, then graphite in the years since. But after a period of emphasis on line speed, old ideas of limp leaders came back, first with the resurgence of twined and furled leaders, then with composites such as the Airflo poly leaders. These leaders, like their gut predecessors, rely almost solely on the momentum of the cast to turn them over.

Regardless of the leader design, you need to put just the right amount of energy into the cast to turn over the leader and fly. If you put too much energy into the cast at the backcast stage, the line may double over on it-self, resulting in loops that may stop the cast from ever having a chance of reaching the target. Too much energy at the end of a cast causes so much recoil that instead of S curves, loops of tangled line result. If you do not put enough energy into the cast, gravity takes over, and the fly hits the water or ground behind you on the backcast.

HINGING

Hinging occurs in fly line or leader when the loop of a cast progresses through a point of high contrast in line flexibility great enough to cause the loop to form a hinge point rather than a smooth transition. The contrast can be in two different materials knotted together or at a connection, such as a loop-to-loop, where the line is not rigid enough to transfer energy effi-ciently. This phenomenon causes diminished energy transfer, at least, and loop collapse in severe cases. The simplest way to minimize hinging is to form gradual transitions rather than abrupt contrasts in flexibility. You can accomplish this in many leader designs by keeping the diameter of successive segments in a taper within about 60 percent of the previous segment, assum-ing the materials are otherwise similar. Exceptions to this are if you prefer to introduce great amounts of slack at the end of the leader to reduce drag, or if you use a specific type of leader with a deliberate hinge in it to accommo-date a float and dropper arrangement, such as the right-angle leader.

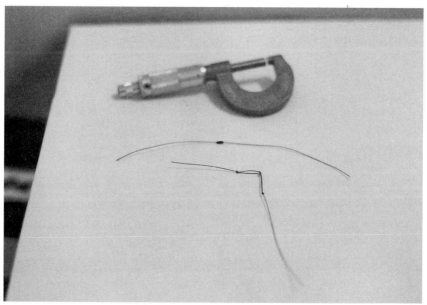

The loop connection (bottom) arranged for a right-angle leader hinge.

A simple means of checking the potential for hinging is to form a loop 2 or 3 inches in circumference with the two joined materials, with the union at the point on the circle opposite your thumb and forefinger. By moving the loop around with your hand, you can see what sort of connection exists. If the loop shape is constant and the curve around the loop is smooth, the connection is efficient. If the connection is angular or flexes more or less than the rest of the loop, there is a good possibility that a hinge exists and you will lose energy at the connection during the cast.

DRAG WITH FLOATING VERSUS SINKING LEADERS

Leaders for most types of fishing should present the fly in a natural state of drag-free drift in the water. Many currents are present at the surface of the water, but there are usually more diverse currents, and more opportunities for drag, below the surface. So a leader that sinks even a small amount is more susceptible to drag than one at the surface.

The extent to which currents may drag the leader also depends on the amount of surface area of the leader in contact with those currents. A leader that has less surface area in direct contact with the water has less potential for drag. A leader that floats on top of the surface has a significantly smaller amount of surface area in contact with the water, because at least half of it is above the water. If you dress a leader with floatant so it rides higher, you can reduce contact to a smaller area still, further minimizing drag. If you dry the leader with false casts, you run the risk of sending a shower of droplets to the surface to signal the fish that something unnatural is about, especially on glassy water or when the sun is out.

Traditionalists have long maintained that fish will not be as leader-shy when encountering materials below the surface, so conventional practice

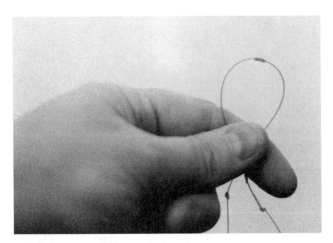

Direct transfer of energy across a blood knot is demonstrated by the smooth loop.

A surgeon's knot creates a less smooth transition, shown by the more angular loop.

has been to strive toward a leader that sinks below the surface, even for dry flies. In fact, an old fly fisherman's toast goes something like this: "May the wind be always fair and at your back, may you never cast a shadow, may the fish always rise, and may your leaders always sink." However, the old philosophy that a leader that sinks just below the surface is better than a floating one is not necessarily appropriate when you want to avoid drag, as when fishing dry flies.

A floating leader creates a distortion in a smooth water surface as it is held up by the surface tension. The combination of the leader and the dimpled trough in the water's surface will at least attract some attention from a trout underneath. So it only seems to make sense to want the leader to sink below the surface, so it does not create this distraction. But in the case of dry flies, you do not want the leader to sink so much that it drags the fly with it, except in cases where you intend to simulate a drowned spinner or emerger near the surface film. The smaller the fly, the greater the tendency for a sinking leader to pull the fly through the surface tension. Fluorocarbon is significantly heavier than nylon, which is heavier than water. So especially for small dry flies on slick water, an untreated nylon tippet may be the best solution, as it will not be so heavy that it will sink and pull the fly along with it. It is also important to retrieve the line in such a way that it does not create such a commotion in the water that it spooks your quarry. This is even more important when the leader sinks, because there is a tendency for the water to hold on to the leader as it is pulled from the stream or lake. A slow, deliberate start to the pickup and backcast, rather than a ripping energy-packed backcast is in order.

Light has a great deal to do with whether a floating leader will be a problem. On bright days on smooth water, the leader will cast a shadow that may appear to a wary trout like a jet's vapor trail in a clear sky. The sight of a linear shadow overhead may not necessarily spook a trout into fleeing, but it may provide just enough of a distraction to prevent the trout from considering your fly as food, particularly if the fly is associated with the unnatural shadow.

Cloudy days or, better yet, days with wind or precipitation minimize the importance of the shadow produced by line and leader. In such conditions, if the trout spends its energy straining to find every deviation from the natural scenery overhead, it won't have time to eat. Then too, clouds, wind, and rain conceal the trout as well as the fisherman, and this may encourage the trout to behave less defensively.

In moving water with some texture to the surface, the disadvantages of a sinking leader may outweigh its advantages. Rippled, moving water, particularly highly turbulent water, has enough surface distortion that the dimpling caused by a floating leader is insignificant to a trout. Such water also has a higher oxygen level, which means a higher metabolism rate for the trout and the need for more food. Finally, the food in such water moves by at a faster rate, so a trout that takes too much time to decide whether to accept or reject an item may lose so many opportunities that he starves.

From the fisherman's standpoint, a sinking leader makes things more difficult. Turbulence is often caused by underwater obstructions, such as large rocks, fallen trees, or other obstacles, and a sinking leader can be pulled into these obstacles and tangle up.

If you want a fly drifting on the surface to appear as natural and unattached to your tackle as possible, a leader that sinks below the surface of turbulent water is a real problem. From the moment the leader sinks into the water, it is traveling at a different speed, and possibly a different direction, than the surface current on which you want the fly to travel. The immediate result is drag, and a wake will be visible downstream of the fly. Mending the line and leader, flipping a slack loop into it to relieve drag, is complicated by the fact that the leader is underwater, and the surface tension now works against you to hold the leader below the surface. The result can be a spray of water, and sometimes more drag than you started with.

So for moving water, a floating leader is preferable for dry flies, regardless of their size. A floating leader, or one treated to float, aids the overall ease of mending, line handling, presentation, and your ability to watch for drag on the fly and the leader and line.

LEADER DESIGN COMPONENTS

From a basic standpoint, a leader is designed to place the fly far enough at the end of the cast that the fish is not alarmed by the fly line or its impact on the water when it lands. The leader also provides a material fine enough to thread through the eye of a hook. A nontapered or flat line will do the job under ideal conditions and will catch fish. But a designed tapered leader will achieve this goal with the added benefits of presenting the fly in both a more energy-efficient and natural fashion, increasing the potential that the fish will take it. A designed leader will continue to transfer the energy of the cast to more efficiently get the fly farther from the end of the line, and for more delicate presentations, it will introduce slack in the form of S curves at the end of the leader to help minimize drag.

Leader diameter is designated with X values. The X values originally were assigned based on the number of times the strands of gut that made up the leaders were pulled through a series of diamond-edged cutters of decreasing size. The more passes through the cutters, the higher the X value and the smaller the diameter. When manufacturers began to use synthetic materials, standard values were assigned to 1X through 10X to keep dimensions constant. In general, the system is based on a material with a diameter of 0.011 inches as 0X. For every 0.001-inch increase in diameter, subtract 1 from the X value; thus 1X = 0.010 inch and 10X = 0.001 inch.

Leader formulas that have appeared in print and on the Internet attributed to various experts are usually presented as recipes, with the lengths of leader material of various diameters assembled from butt to tip. Some formulas, notably those in English or European literature, are given using the breaking strength in pounds-test of various materials used, which makes some sort of conversion necessary when substituting materials. These formulas were more than adequate when there were few leader and tippet manufacturers, as a person could customize a particular design by using one material or another. But there are now dozens of different makers of leader materials, and the consistency of these materials in diameter and flexibility varies with individual companies. And, as one company buys or absorbs another, the materials may change or be replaced by new ones. So it becomes necessary to characterize the materials by their properties regardless of their maker, in order to continue to make leaders that will suit anglers' needs without having to reinvent the formulas each time a material is discontinued or changed.

Most designed leaders consist of three components, starting at the end of the fly line: the energy transfer taper, the transition taper, and the presentation section, which includes the tippet. The energy transfer taper (or butt) continues to smoothly transfer the energy of the cast and turns over in a loop close to the shape of the fly line. The transition taper (or simply taper) slows the speed of the fly and leader so that they do not hit the water with a high impact splash. The presentation section slows the speed of the loop until it unfolds, and often presents the fly at the end of a series of S curves, allowing the leader to resist drag. The tippet is the last segment of the presentation section and is the defense against detection, presenting the fly at the end of a fine line that will fall with enough slack to reduce drag.

The distinctions among these elements are not always clear. Some leaders lack one or more of these components. Leader formulas have been produced over the years based on the ratios of the components without necessarily referring to them by these names. Some authors refer to tippets and butt sections as separate from the designed portion of the leader, possibly referring only to the tapered portion as the leader, creating possible semantic confusion. Other descriptions refer to the parts of the leader as the butt, taper, and tippet, implying in the simplest case that the stiff butt segment and thinnest tippet segment are not multiple segments, and the taper is everything in between. Descriptions become even less clear when these designs use tapered butt sections and tippets that are made of materials of more than one diameter.

Numerous experts have endorsed a general-purpose leader with a 60-20-20 formula, which means that 60 percent of the leader is stiffer energy transfer material, and both the transition and presentation tapers are 20 percent of the total length. The 60-20-20 formula is attributed to Charles Ritz, who published his notions in the 1950 printing of *A Fly Fisher's Life*. Ritz also proposed that the butt section—the first section of the energy transfer taper—should have a diameter approximately 60 percent that of the tip of the fly line. This 60 percent idea has continued, although Ritz was working with silk lines and gut leaders, and modern synthetic-coated lines tend to be thicker and lighter than the old silk materials. And in contrast to early silk fly lines, the coatings on new fly lines may vary greatly in flexibility from one maker to another.

You may actually see the casting loop open up slightly at a line-leader transition in which the diameter of the leader butt section is 60 percent the diameter of the line tip. This is because most fly lines lighter than 5-weight are more supple than a similar thickness of nylon leader material. In other words, nylon at 60 percent of the line diameter may actually be stiffer than the line. If you do not observe this phenomenon, it may be that your first energy transfer segment is supple enough, or your cast has enough loop speed that momentum keeps the loop geometry relatively constant. Another possibility is that enough energy is lost or dissipated at the connection between the leader and line that the loop continues at the same size or smaller.

There are also 40-20-40 formulas, which may have developed since the introduction of nylon and may be more appropriate in general to modern materials. Many efforts have been made to reduce all leaders to simple ratios like this, but oversimplification may not always be the best approach. Different people cast differently, and circumstances such as wind and water speed are highly variable as well. And the definition of each section of the leader may differ among individuals, appearing to alter the ratio but actually just redefining the terms. Many people who have endorsed the 60-20-20 formula have gone on to give examples that do not hold up to the definitions indicated above; however, what matters in the end is whether they work.

The Energy Transfer Taper
The energy transfer taper should be designed to maintain enough velocity in the loop to extend the trajectory beyond the end of the fly line. You can achieve this by using a leader with a butt segment that has physical properties close to those of the end of the fly line, and attaching the two materials with an energy-efficient connection. You can also accomplish this by using a leader with an energy transfer section that has sufficient mass to maintain the forward momentum of the loop. So a more flexible material of sufficient weight can maintain the speed of the loop just as well as a lighter but stiffer material. If the energy transfer taper is much stiffer than the line, it can actually open up the loop and cause the leader to turn over prematurely or whip in an uncontrolled fashion. This is usually not noticed, because the union of the two materials tends to result in energy loss at the knot or loop connection. But it can and does happen.

The 60 percent rule used with the more common lines and leaders will minimize hinging but may cause casting loops to open. In most recipes today, the butt of the energy transfer taper is typically less than 60 percent the diameter of the end of the fly line, as most fly lines are made of plastic materials that are more flexible than monofilament leader materials. The contrast between these materials can be minimized by a reduction in the diameter of the butt of the leader. Here are some general guidelines for butt section size and line weight:

Leader Butt Size by Line Weight

Line Weight	Butt Size
1 or 2	0.017 in.
3 or 4	0.019 in.
5 or 6	0.021 in.
6 or 7	0.022 in.
8 or 9	0.023 in.

You may need to adjust these sizes to compensate for the type of fly used or field and wind conditions. Heavily weighted nymphs or high winds may require larger-diameter butt sections; midge fishing or delicate spring creek presentations might call for a reduction in size. And the leader used for sparsely hackled #16 dry flies is likely too limp for a heavily hackled #16 Wulff pattern.

The energy transfer taper is generally twice the diameter of the tippet or greater, and it is characteristically made of stiffer material than the rest of the leader. It does not taper steeply; the difference between the diameter of the two ends is usually less than 25 percent, and the length of the sections is generally longer—more than 10 inches and up to 6 feet or longer.

The Transition Taper

The transition taper is the portion of the leader between the energy transfer taper and the presentation section, where the bulk of the reduction in diameter occurs. It is made up of segments generally shorter than the energy transfer taper and the final tippet.

The transition taper must continue to convey the loop toward the fly while slowing the fly down so that it does not spin into a spiral or snap like a whip when the loop reaches it in the backcast. This is accomplished by gradually softening the leader, usually by reducing the diameter in a series of segments of progressively finer material, so that the energy transfer becomes less and less efficient. For most applications, this is the portion of the leader that begins to produce the S curves needed to reduce drag during the fly's drift. The use of shorter segments in this part of the leader helps induce the formation of S curves, and the energy loss from multiple splices slows the fly.

The transition taper may be shorter than the other two sections, yet it may have more sections and more knots to tie. One way to simplify this section is to substitute a section of tapered knotless leader with the same starting and ending diameter as the transition taper in the recipe you have chosen. This will reduce the need for knots, and because knotless tapered leaders are often made of material that is neither very hard nor very soft, as the manufacturers want to cover a wide range of applications, they may be well suited for this transitional portion of the leader. The length of the tapered segment of a knotless leader will be longer than the same section of a tied leader, because the extrusion process cannot easily produce a steep taper over a short length. Consequently, if you use this method, your overall leader may be longer.

The Presentation Section

The presentation section is the portion of the leader designed to present the fly in the most natural fashion possible. This includes production of slack line necessary to avoid current drag and slowing of the loop speed to the extent that the fly lands on the water surface with either minimal (as in the case of dry flies) or the desired amount (as with nymphs or streamers) of impact. The presentation taper is also thinner than the rest of the leader in order to avoid spooking fish and to promote the formation of drag-resistant S curves.

The presentation section of the leader generally consists of the last two longer segments of finer-diameter material: the tippet and the section of the leader between it and the transition taper. Segments in the presentation taper are generally longer than the transition taper segments. You can vary the length of the tippet as a means of fine-tuning the leader to compensate for varying conditions of water and wind. Tippet sizes are typically based on the size or wind resistance of the fly. In general, you should increase the diameter of the tippet if you intend to add split shot, to accommodate the additional stress during casting and the potential for weakening the material when pinching on the weight. You may also wish to upsize and/or shorten the tippet to accommodate bushy wind-resistant dry flies or where a high degree of stealth is not required, such as in turbid water.

Recommended Tippet Sizes for Various Hook Sizes

Hook or Fly Size	Tippet Size
0, 1, 2 (weighted or not)	0.011 in. (0X)
4, 6, 8 (weighted or not)	0.010 in. (1X)
6, 8, 10 (weighted or not)	0.009 in. (2X)
10, 12, 14 (weighted or not)	0.008 in. (3X)
12 (unweighted), 14, 16 (weighted or not)	0.007 in. (4X)
14, 16, 18 (weighted or not)	0.006 in. (5X)
16, 18, 20, 22 (weighted or not)	0.005 in. (6X)

Schematic of Leader Sections

Schematic of a typical tapered leader, showing proportions of segments.

These guidelines do not mean that you must change your tippet every time you change fly size. They are general guidelines that will optimize casting and your presentation under most conditions.

In summary: basic leader design includes an **energy transfer section** capable of efficiently carrying the energy of the cast from the line to the leader, a **transition taper** to slow loop speed and aid in controlling presentation, and a **presentation section** to gently present the fly.

CHAPTER 5

Basic Leader Construction

MATERIALS

Leader materials and the knots or connections between segments have evolved over time. You can adjust the performance of leaders by selecting materials or connections, or both, to suit varying conditions.

Gut

The discussions in *The Compleat Angler* and other historical works on fly fishing describe leaders made of several different materials. Walton's method used horsehair, as it was a long, thin, single-strand material that could be twined into leaders of relatively high strength to diameter ratio. Later writers described leaders made of catgut, presumed by some to be derived from the gut of silkworms (caterpillars). The presumption that cat-cut was derived exclusively from caterpillars—or cats, for that matter—is very likely inaccurate. Close inspection of any catgut-strung tennis racket would reveal that it would have to have come from a caterpillar well beyond a size that would willingly surrender its entrails in the interest of man's sport. And the likelihood that cats would be used for such a purpose is remote, indeed. Ray Bergman, in *Trout,* says that gut is the excretion of the silk gland of a silkworm, which solidifies on exposure to air and is then drawn to the appropriate diameter.

Whatever its source, gut had a combination of desirable properties that included suppleness and a high strength-to-diameter ratio, and it was either colorless or of an inconspicuous neutral cast of white or tan. It had the distinct disadvantage that it had to be kept wet or damp to retain its suppleness; if it dried out too much, it could be damaged irreparably. Gut leaders were normally stored in a closed container with a moist cloth. Some fishermen used additives on the cloth to help float or sink the leaders and would then have a couple of specially prepared leaders on hand for whatever conditions they encountered. Gut was not cheap, so a fisherman often used the same leaders for several seasons.

Gut leaders were often tied by the individual from presized segments and recipes. The source of the gut limited the length of each segment, and a 20-inch segment was considered extraordinary and was expensive. These considerations limited the recipes to segments between 15 and 20 inches or less.

Silk

Silk was a natural progression from gut, as it has the same or greater strength and suppleness but does not require quite the same level of care. Silk had the added benefit of being more readily available in essentially infinite lengths. To be useful as a floating leader, silk leaders require dressing with a waterproofing agent, preferably with a high surface tension, which will aid in flotation. Although not common, silk is still used in leaders today, particularly in construction of twined or furled leaders.

Monofilament Materials

Monofilament simply refers to materials that have a single strand. Both nylon and fluorocarbon materials are monofilament, as they are single-strand synthetic copolymers, a kind of plastic. Both are nonbiodegradable in the long term, meaning that they will not decompose in the environment, although nylon loses many of its desirable properties. Thus it is important to dispose of any waste materials appropriately as waterfowl and fish can become tangled in fishing line or leaders and die.

Nylon

Nylon was the first totally synthetic fiber material. The original Fiber #66 was developed in the late 1930s, and Du Pont built the first nylon manufacturing plant in 1939, starting a synthetic fiber revolution in the United States. Modifications to the original recipe were made to increase or decrease the flexibility and density of the polymer, primarily through its absorption of water. Nylon is a high-strength plastic copolymer compound that became especially popular after World War II as a fishing line material. Rather than a single specific compound, nylon includes any of a variety of compounds that can be combined to optimize the desired properties. It can be easily colored in the manufacturing process, and consistent quality control in its manufacture is not a major problem. Nylon has specific gravity values in the range of 1.05 to 1.25, compared with 1.0 for water, that can be modified by the blend of nylon types used. This fact, combined with a moderately high surface tension, makes it a good choice for dry-fly leaders where flotation is important. It can be used untreated and will hold very close to the water's surface because it is so close to the density of water, or it can be treated with agents to make it sink or float.

Nylon will absorb water, and its specific gravity and modulus of elasticity both become lower as it absorbs more water. So even if you compare samples of nylon material in a store or at home in dry conditions, you may not be simulating on-stream conditions. Nylon should be stored dry, as moisture will hasten the rate at which it loses strength and becomes brittle.

Nylon line is manufactured by several different companies internationally, and one supplier may provide lines for several companies, while tailoring the characteristics to each company's particular recipe. Nylon beads are fed into an extruder and pulled through to the desired diameter or taper. Plasticizers are added before extrusion to modify the hardness of the nylon, typically by modifying the amount of water that nylon will absorb. Heat also tends to soften nylon. In practice, the stiffness of nylon will then depend on its absorption of water and the temperature.

As it is the most popular material for fishing line today, nylon monofilament line is available in nearly every diameter and color a fisherman is likely to use. It is typically sold based on the manufacturer's strength rating, which is often conservative so the consumer will not be unpleasantly surprised by breakage. Nylon that is packaged and sold for leaders is usually labeled with the diameter as well as the strength rating. European leader formulas typically give the manufacturer's strength rating of segments,

Selecting materials can be confusing. Don't hesitate to ask the owner of the fly shop for assistance, if you need it.

whereas American ones generally use the diameter. One manufacturer may choose to market its 5X nylon as 3.3-pounds-test, while another may want to hedge its bets and say that the strength is only 2.5-pounds-test. In reality, they may be the same strength, or the 2.5-pound-test material may actually be stronger than the 3.3-pound-test material. In addition, manufacturers' diameter measurements are not always accurate; so one maker's 5X may actually be 4X or 6X. Fortunately, manufacturers at least tend to be consistent in their measurements, so the taper will still progress, but maybe not with the diameters you might expect. To determine that the materials are appropriate for the leader you want to assemble, you may have to use a micrometer or some other means of getting an accurate measurement.

As nylon ages, it will become weak and brittle in response to heat and ultraviolet light. Nylon also tends to absorb water. For these reasons, you should store nylon line in dry, dark containers.

Fluorocarbon

Fluorocarbons were "invented" as an accidental combination of plastics in a container of tetrafluoroethylene gas being investigated as an alternative to Freon refrigerants in 1938. The original polymer was extraordinary in its low-friction characteristics. Subsequent developments and modifications to the accidental polymer added desirable properties, including resistance to water, ultraviolet light, and chemical degradation. Fluorocarbon materials have been around for some time in fishing and have found their way into fly fishing as a special-use item.

Fluorocarbon refers to a group of plastic polymers that include fluorine in their molecular structure and are marketed under various descriptions, including abbreviations for the chemical compounds, such as PTFE (polytetrafluorethylene, or Teflon) and PVDF (polyvinylidenfluoride, or Kynar). Like most polymers, fluorocarbons can be manufactured with a wide range of physical properties through the use of plasticizers and other additives. The fluorocarbon compounds used in monofilament have refractive indexes—the optical property that describes the behavior of light as it passes through different materials—similar to that of water. Materials with contrasting refractive indexes reflect light at their interface as glare. For materials with similar refractive indexes, more light passes through the interface, and less light is reflected as glare. The less glare, the less visibility. What this means to a fisherman is that this material becomes nearly invisible below the water's surface, because the boundary between it and the water does not reflect as much light.

When viewed under a microscope in water, equivalent diameters of clear nylon and fluorocarbon appear similar. When the samples are backlit, as a fish would see them—light from above the water would pass through the materials in water—a couple of differences become evident. Both materials exhibit a concentrated stripe of light, possibly the focused internally reflected light; however, the band is narrower in the fluorocarbon line. This may be because more of the light is transmitted through the fluorocarbon material without refraction or reflection. It is possible that the width of this light stripe is significant, but there is little reason to believe fish will care whether the band is 30 or 50 microns thick—it is there in both cases. Most of the nylon monofilament samples examined tended to show more surface dirt and scratches than the fluorocarbon samples. This could be a function of surface tension or static, but the difference may have some significance.

Fluorocarbon monofilament is heavier than nylon, having a specific gravity in the range of 1.65 to 2.0, or twice that of water, and thus it has more of a tendency to sink than nylon. But fluorocarbon has a relatively high surface tension, so it may tend to be caught for a brief period of time on the surface of the water. Once it breaks through the surface tension, pulled by a weighted fly, or by turbulence or the force of impact, it will tend to sink on its own, but it can be treated with a floatant to keep it afloat a little longer. The downside of using treatments on fluorocarbon is that they may alter the optical property that is touted by manufacturers as a major advantage over nylon. Because of these characteristics, it is generally best suited for wet-fly or nymph presentations or as a tippet material. If it is used for the entire leader, its tendency to sink may make it difficult to

A microscopic view of fluorocarbon (top) and nylon (bottom) 5X tippet material in dirty water, lit from behind the slide. This is how these materials might appear to a fish underwater. Compare the differences in the surfaces, the amount of dirt that clings to the two materials, and their overall visibility.

mend, and if the mending has to extend into the leader, drag will have already occurred. An entire leader constructed of fluorocarbon may be heavy enough to sink any but the most buoyant or bushy dry fly. The weight of fluorocarbon leaders also makes them more prone to straightening out during a cast, so it may be necessary to adjust your casting stroke to attain the desired S curves.

Fluorocarbon is similar to nylon though slightly softer, and the two can be combined if you join them with proper knots. A double surgeon's knot is usually sufficient to hold the two materials together, if you moisten the knot before tightening. Closely related to the compound used in nonstick cookware, fluorocarbon tends to be more slippery than nylon, having a lower coefficient of static friction. Another advantage of fluorocarbon leaders is their resistance to ultraviolet light degradation. Fluorocarbon is also tougher than nylon in that it is more abrasion resistant and less brittle. This is due in part to its slickness, as the line slides over rocks and obstacles with less resistance than nylon, reducing abrasion. Thus it is often used in subsurface leaders where abrasion is a consideration.

Polyurethane

Polyurethane plastics were developed initially as alternatives to natural latex rubber. Early production in Germany in the late 1930s was directed at military uses for the material. Following World War II, the Bayer Company marketed two polyurethane formulas: Igamid, for general plastics; and Perion, for synthetic fibers. Polyurethane copolymers are, in general, highly elastic, meaning great flexibility, and they will readily stretch before breaking, much like latex, which they were developed to replace. As with most polymers, a wide variety of their physical properties can be modified by additives and processing temperatures and pressure.

Polyurethane is useful in leader materials because of its highly flexible nature. It is more supple than either nylon or fluorocarbon and can be manufactured as hybrid polymers, by using additives or modifying the curing process, with densities less than or greater than that of water. It can be modified by additives to resist degradation by ultraviolet light and ozone, and it is essentially waterproof, so its properties are not changed by absorbing water.

Composite Materials

Manufacturers are experimenting with an increasing number of composite materials for leaders, possibly as a result of the market successes of new fly line materials and designs. Airflo currently markets multimaterial poly leaders that have properties very different from those of conventional nylon leaders. One innovation is the combination of polyurethane and other synthetic polymers with nylon. Because of their softness, polyurethane and other lightweight polymers do not have good strand or knot strength by themselves, so these leaders may be manufactured with a fluorocarbon or a monofilament, composite core.

In a composite leader, the stronger nylon-cored material forms a loop connection at the butt, and then the outer material tapers to negligible thickness or ends altogether at the tip, where an additional nylon tippet may be knotted on. Provided the core is of adequate strength, the leaders may be tapered based on weight and stiffness rather than strength, so that the only factors in the design become performance in the cast and in the drift.

The composite design results in leaders that may be closer in flexibility to that of silk or of the traditional gut leaders used by Ritz. The suppleness of these leaders is so great that they maintain loop shape and speed effectively through the connection between line and leader by virtue of the line's momentum, rather than stiffness of the energy transfer section, turning the line over effectively in tight, high-speed loops. This line speed is a great asset in windy situations and where casting into a tight spot surrounded by brush requires small, tight loops. Conventional leaders have used the stiffness of nylon to transfer the energy of the cast, but the supple nature of the poly leaders maintains momentum not by loading and unloading the stiff energy transfer section, but rather by maintaining the velocity of the loop through the initial section of the leader. By being more supple than conventional leaders, composite or poly leaders also deform more readily than conventional leaders in response to multiple currents, thereby fighting the effects of drag in the water.

The coaxial composite material leader concept allows the construction of leaders that are either lighter than water, so they float, or significantly heavier than water, permitting them to sink without adding lead or other more visible weights. This may be done using fluorocarbon or other materials of greater density than nylon, and some tungsten-impregnated leaders on the market are as much as three to four times the density of water.

One trait observed with coaxial composites is delamination. The elongation properties of the core materials are dissimilar to those of the more flexible copolymers, such as polyurethane or polyethylene, used in the outer sleeve. When the leader is stretched, either when the fisherman straightens it out or by a fish on the line, the fact that the two materials stretch at different rates may cause them to shear longitudinally. When this happens, the core may become free to move within the sleeve of the outer material, and a portion of the softer outer material can separate from the core. Any minor surface projection from the delamination is likely to be

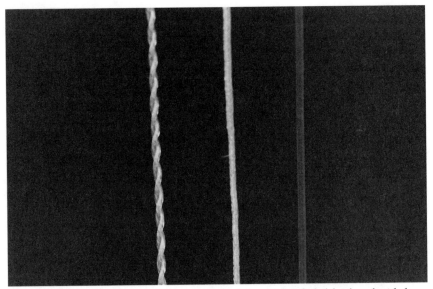

Alternatives to monofilament leaders include (left to right) furled leaders, braided leaders, and poly leaders.

less than the size of most knots and is not regarded as a problem. Delamination may not be a problem unless the leader relies on the strength of both core and outer material for its total strength.

The coaxial leaders designed for near-surface or subsurface presentation tend to be optically designed for stealth, combined with a level of suppleness that allows the leader to respond to various contrasting currents with less drag than a stiff leader. Because wet flies and nymphs are generally less wind-resistant and may be weighted, they cast quite well in spite of the limpness of these leaders, and after adjusting the stroke slightly to the difference, one can easily turn over most flies with these products. Casting with larger dry flies may be a different story, and again, some adjustment in casting stroke may be necessary. Regardless, the suppleness of these leaders can result in excessively straight-line presentations, and you should ensure that the cast has a high enough level of energy to allow some recoil and S curve formation before the line hits the water.

Some Thoughts on Combining Materials

Some of us cannot leave well enough alone. If something works fine, we try to tweak it a little and see if it can be made even better. Sometimes curiosity, rather than necessity, is the mother of invention. But some pre-experimental thought can save time in the creative process. There can be advantages, as well as problems, to using different materials for different parts of the leader. You can choose the material for each section to provide the best balance of advantages and disadvantages, while emphasizing the primary purpose of that part of the leader.

The energy transfer section can be made up of any material that efficiently transfers the energy of the cast from the line to the leader without being too conspicuous in its appearance. If the leader is designed to float, the material should be close to the specific gravity of water, so nylon and the floating poly leader composites are candidates. For sinking leader designs, consider fluorocarbon, sinking poly leader composite, or nylon treated to sink. So how can you refine your selection? If your casting style is based on high line speeds and tight loops, the efficiency of a poly leader type energy transfer section may be preferable. These leaders maintain line speed by being so flexible that the size of the casting loop may actually compress from the line through the energy transfer section. The advantages are accuracy and the ability to penetrate wind and cast into tight situations. The disadvantages are that the manufacturer sells only limited sizes and lengths of these products, you have to control the speed to avoid line slap, and the leader must have a suitable transition section to develop S curves in the presentation section or the cast will be straight.

Nylon is available with the widest variety of properties—sizes, colors, and degrees of flexibility—meaning that it can give you the widest range of characteristics for the energy transfer section. For sinking leaders, fluorocarbon has the advantages of stealth and strength, as well as being available in various diameters, unlike the sinking poly leader products. The sinking poly leader products, on the other hand, are available in several densities, allowing different sink rates.

The transition section should be designed to complement the other sections of the leader, as well as to provide a transition from energy transfer to delicacy of presentation. It is awkward to go from one material in the energy transfer section to another in the transition section, and then either back to the first material in the presentation section or to yet a third material. The physical properties of the transition section should be appropriate to the task at hand—slowing the loop down without collapsing it or sending the cast into chaos. For floating leaders, a transition section works best for most casting styles if it is the same type of material as the energy transfer section. This simplifies knots and limits you to a reasonable number of spools in your vest. The knotless taper from a knotless leader may be used for this section as well. In the poly products, the transition section is predesigned into the leader. For sinking leaders, it is not as easy to go from fluorocarbon energy transfer to nylon transition taper, because the energy transfer section will have a higher sink rate, causing drift problems and adding to the awkwardness of pickup and retrieve. For heavily weighted poly leaders, the transition section is nonexistent.

The presentation section is where creativity can be important. The poly leader products are designed to attach a presentation section of monofilament nylon or fluorocarbon, depending on whether you want the tippet to sink or float. The same logic applies to nylon and fluorocarbon leaders: Use nylon if you want the tippet to float and fluorocarbon if you want it to sink. The lengths of the segments depend on the design of the leader and the conditions of the stream. Braided and furled leaders are designed to perform the energy transfer and transition functions. A presentation section of nylon or fluorocarbon is added using the same considerations for flotation as in other leaders. Poly, furled, and braided leaders, in that order, use higher line speed (highest for poly leaders) and momentum to get the cast to the target. Unless you adjust your casting technique to incorporate a wiggle at the end or recoil S curves, the presentation section used with these leaders should be longer than for a conventional monofilament leader to allow the development of more S curves to counter the effect of a high-speed straight-line cast. In the long run, this can be an advantage in stealth and overall presentation.

CONNECTIONS

It is nearly impossible to fish consistently well without knowing how to tie a few basic knots. Poorly tied knots can and will lose fish. But properly tied knots will help a well-designed leader produce the desired trajectory and achieve proper presentation. Bulky knots will add to the wind resistance of a leader and may also add weight, which may cause surface disturbance on impact. A great deal has been written on the various types of knots and how they affect the overall strength of a leader; however, a properly tied knot will diminish the ultimate breaking strength of a leader by only a small percentage. More often, breaks that occur at or near the knot are the result of overtensioning the knot; kinking or nicking of the line, causing a weak spot; or the incomplete set of a knot tied with dry line.

The only way to become proficient with knots is practice. Just as some fly tiers start each session with larger flies and work their way down to smaller ones, to allow their eyes and fingers time to adapt to smaller flies, you may want to start practicing tying knots using clothesline, working your way down to monofilament. A couple lengths of old fly line make good materials to practice with; it is not as bulky as clothesline but is large enough to allow reasonable inspection of the knot. This will not only allow you to gain familiarity with the knots, but will also allow you to see the way the line should wrap in the knot as it is tightened. Lubricate all knots to facilitate tightening. In general, it is a good idea to use connections that continue the transfer of energy across the two materials as efficiently as possible, particularly in the energy transfer and transition taper.

Line to Leader

The connection between line and leader is critical to the efficiency of a leader, and there are dozens of methods to accomplish this connection. If the connection is not tight, it may result in hinging at the joint, and much of the effort that went into a well-designed leader and a good cast will have been wasted. In spite of the relative diameters, the large difference between the weight of a fly line and the energy transfer taper of a leader may compensate for an inefficient connection, and a loose connection may only slightly decrease loop speed under some conditions. Wind and the type of cast may also affect the degree to which this holds true, as the speed of the line in a shooting cast may make the efficiency of the line-to-leader connection a trivial concern.

Among the most common ways to join line to leader is the loop-to-loop connection. When the loops are tightened sufficiently, this can be a reasonably good connection, and it affords great ease in changing leaders. This requires that the loops be between ³/₄ and 1 inch in length. Larger sizes result in loops that tend to open and loosen. Smaller loops may be too small to easily interconnect, as the knots hang up on each other, and the loops are difficult to manage.

The strongest and most efficient connection between fly line and leader is a needle knot, which allows the line-to-leader connection to behave as though the two materials are one by aligning the two materials concentrically. To tie the knot, first soften the line in either hot water or a solvent such as acetone, a component of most fingernail polish removers; insert a needle through the tip of the fly line; and poke a hole approximately ¹/₂ inch from the tip. Then insert the butt of the leader, pull it out through the hole, and tie it to the line as shown.

The needle knot provides a low-relief connection that easily travels through the guides. The first segment of the energy transfer taper is likely

Loop-to-Loop Connection

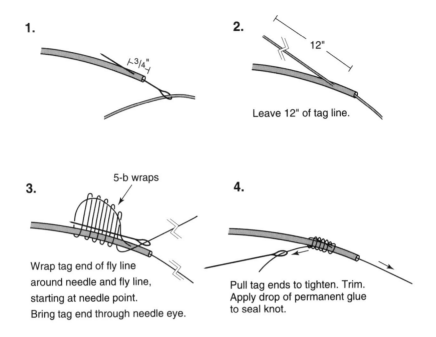

1.

3/4"

2.

12"

Leave 12" of tag line.

3.

5-b wraps

Wrap tag end of fly line
around needle and fly line,
starting at needle point.
Bring tag end through needle eye.

4.

Pull tag ends to tighten. Trim.
Apply drop of permanent glue
to seal knot.

Needle Knot

to be the same diameter, regardless of leader type, so attaching a 15- to 20-inch length of properly selected monofilament acts as the initial segment of the energy transfer taper, regardless of the rest of the leader. Energy transfer becomes secondary to presentation quality toward the tip of the leader. So tying a loop in the end of the first or even the second segment of the leader allows attachment of subsequent segments without knots at a point where energy transfer is less essential than at the union of two very different materials, the line and leader. If you use a high-visibility material for the thickest part of the energy transfer taper, it acts as a low-impact strike or drag indicator as well.

Another low-profile connection between the line and leader is the Zap-a-Gap or Krazy Glue (cyanoacrylate) union. To make this connection, first soften the coating of the fly line using a mild solvent such as acetone or toluene. Solvent is preferable to hot water for this purpose, as it does not affect the bonding of the glue and the line. This connection is not

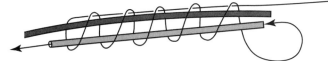

Make 5–6 loops over tube and lines.

Remove tube. Pull tag ends to tighten. Apply a coat of Flex-a-ment.

Tube Nail Knot

recommended for fluorocarbon leaders, because fluorocarbon is so resistant to solvents and has such a low friction coefficient that it does not bind well with glues or solvents. Dip only the tip—less than 1 inch—of the line into the solvent, and keep it there for about thirty seconds. Once the coating is softened, you can easily strip off the outer coating of the fly line with your fingernails, leaving only the woven core material. Insert a needle in the tip to open the core material back to the coated portion of the line. While leaving the tip of the needle in the core material to maintain the opening, roughen the butt of the leader with a fingernail file. Then cut the butt of the leader at an angle to facilitate insertion of the fly line into the core. Remove the needle, and push the butt of the leader into the core of the fly line beyond the stripped section and into the coated section. Put a drop of Krazy Glue or Zap-a-Gap on the butt section where it is covered by the fly-line core, and the woven material will wick the glue into the tip of the fly line. Place the connection on the edge of a surface where the glue will not attach it to anything else while it sets. After five minutes, check the connection for strength by gradually pulling on it. This type of connection has no knot, as such, and relies on the strength of the glue bond. If the surface of the butt section is not properly roughened and the connection fails, the leader will pull out. Such failures may be catastrophic; make frequent pull tests after the initial connection.

A third low-profile connection is the no-knot eyelet or similar add-on connections. This type of connection amounts to the insertion of a barbed eyelet into the end of the fly line. The eyelet is essentially the barbed shank and eyelet of a bait hook, minus the bend and point. The barbs keep the eyelet from backing out of the fly line. You simply tie the leader into the eyelet with a clinch knot or surgeon's loop. The ease of this connection is obvious. The downside of it is that in time, the eyelet will wear on the interior of the line, likely breaking free with the fish of a lifetime. The connection is also more dense than a knot or a glue connection and will sink in the water more readily.

Braided butt sections with loops are marketed by different line companies for connecting lines to leaders. These connections are convenient, once attached, but also have disadvantages. The braided butt section is hollow and slides over the fly line. To use one, you fit a sleeve of plastic shrink-wrap material, much like the coating of the fly line, over the connection and heat it so that it shrinks and bonds the line and leader. Tension on the braided butt section will constrict the braid, adding to the strength of the bond. Problems may arise when the braided section is repeatedly stressed and released. The braided section may work its way loose, stretching the outer sleeve, and may slip off the line. Make frequent inspections to prevent this from occurring at the worst possible time. Another disadvantage of the braided butt connection is that it collects water in the braided section under surface tension. When the cast is made, the water in the braided section is released as spray, which may cause enough surface disturbance to spook the fish. Also, the combined weight of the braided monofilament and the outer sleeve can make the connection heavy enough to sink the tip of a floating fly line, especially with lighter line weights.

Leader Material to Leader Material

A few considerations determine which knot is best to use where in the leader, or where you are doing the tying. There is a big difference between tying blood knots in midstream, with water pulling you downstream, wind, and marginal lighting, and tying them under ideal conditions such as you might have at the fly-tying bench. You may tie a less than ideal knot for the situation when tying under field conditions. The time and difficulty involved in tying blood knots or more complicated knots are sometimes a deterrent to using the best knot for the situation.

Much has been written about the difficulties of tying knots between different materials. Some writers recommend using the same manufacturer's material throughout a leader to maintain consistency of knot strength. My suspicion is that many difficulties in knot strength are more a function of overage nylon rather than any incompatibility between materials. But there is a possibility that harder materials will cut into softer materials and cause knots to fail where the materials are thinnest. And a difference in slickness might influence how well or how completely a knot tightens. When in doubt, run a couple simple experiments with different materials. Close inspection of the knot and pull-testing it before casting can save you a lot of frustration later.

Take into consideration both the pluses and minuses when deciding what knot to use. If you tie the wrong knot, you may not present the fly as well to the fish. And even if you make a good presentation, a hastily tied or inappropriate knot may fail should you hook the fish. Then you will have to retie the leader, with the added frustration at having lost the fish that was your target. You also may have spooked other potential quarry by the disturbance made when hooking or losing the fish.

The shape of knots may be a factor in your choice as well. With some knots, such as the blood knot, the line direction does not change from one segment to the next and is essentially straight. These knots tend to transfer energy most efficiently. Other knots, such as the surgeon's knot, introduce an angle of deflection. These knots tend to force the line into a series of bends, which is a desired effect in the presentation section. The surgeon's knot is also easy to tie, and you are far more likely to be retying sections of the presentation section of the leader than the energy transfer or transition taper section.

The most common, yet seemingly difficult, knot to use in leaders is the blood knot. With practice, you can tie it with a moderate level of difficulty.

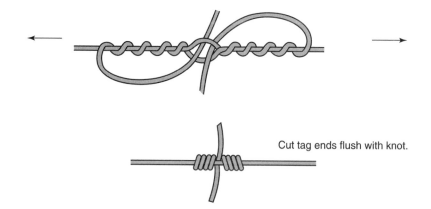

Cut tag ends flush with knot.

Blood Knot
(Also known as Barrel Knot)

Used to join mono of similar size

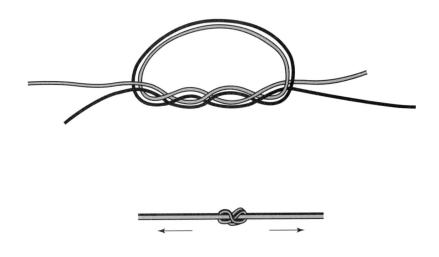

Surgeon's Knot

Easy to tie, very strong, somewhat bulky

It is the most durable knot for leaders, and its low-relief profile is fine for casting and passing through the guides of a rod. The standard blood knot is not as reliable when tied between two contrasting line types or sizes. Gary Borger is credited with modifying the conventional blood knot to more effectively join lines of widely different diameters. He achieved greater degrees of symmetry and strength by using more wraps on the side of the knot with the thinner material. The additional wraps result in more friction, compensating for the smaller-diameter line.

The surgeon's knot is another good, strong knot to attach leader materials. It is much easier to tie but results in a bulkier knot, which is more prone to collect algae and vegetation and to snag on guides. It has the distinct advantage of being strong and reliable, regardless of the types of lines being joined. For this reason, it is commonly used for making quick changes in tippets or in quickly tying a streamer or nighttime leader. The bulkiness of the knot is not so much a concern in the finer materials of the presentation section, as the smaller the material, the smaller the size of the knot.

Loop Connections

The loop-to-loop connections used by many fishermen are quick and easy ways to connect line within the leader. The loops should be tied with an effective knot such as the surgeon's loop, the perfection loop, or nonslip loop. Before casting, test the strength of the loops and trim the stubs of line, then pull the connection tightly together.

Loops have two major potential drawbacks. First, they tend to hinge (bend at a sharp angle) when they loosen. They will not disconnect, but the hinging can prevent smooth turnover or energy transfer in your cast. Second, looped connections create wind resistance, particularly with stiffer materials, and loosening adds still more wind resistance. The more loops, the greater the wind resistance, and the more your leader will be suscepti-ble to crosswinds.

Proper sizing of the loops reduces the potential of loosening but does not entirely eliminate it. The smallest cross section possible for a loop con-nection is twice the line diameter, but that is simply not realistic. Keeping the size between $1/2$ and $3/4$ inch will minimize both wind resistance and hinging. Looping the ends through each other is also important in

Non slip Loop

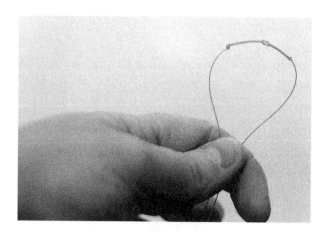

The loop-to-loop connection used in the right-angle leader will hinge, as demon-strated when a section of jointed line is held in a bend.

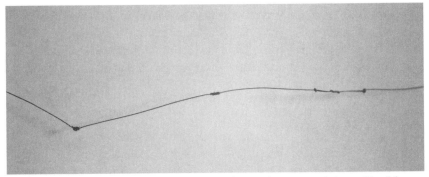

A single leader with different connections. Left to right: surgeon's knot, blood knot, and loop-to-loop connection. Note the angle of the line at the surgeon's knot compared with the blood knot.

reducing the profile of the connection. If only one side of the connection is looped, the connection will actually widen. If both are tucked in, the profile will become slimmer when pulled tight.

Loops are not practical connections in the transition taper of the leader because of the short segments and frequent connections. The loops for this part of the leader would dominate the geometry more than the taper characteristics in terms of the effect on both casting, due to wind resistance, and drag, because so many loops would effectively double the stiffness of the tapered section.

A loop connection can be used to facilitate quick changes, particularly at the leader-to-line connection. Many commercial leaders are fitted with loops at one or both ends to attach to a loop at the line or to add tippet. When used at the leader-to-line connection, the weight and momentum of the entire leader and fly may provide enough tension to maintain a tight connection and minimize hinging. Adjusting your casts to add speed at the forward stroke can also maintain a solid connection.

Loops in the presentation section can add to the ability of this part of the leader to form S curves; however, this advantage may be outweighed by the effects a large number of loops might have on the aerodynamics and hydraulics of a delicate presentation section.

Tippet to Hook

The clinch knot and improved clinch knot are the two most common knots used for attaching the tippet to the fly. The improved clinch knot begins the same as the standard clinch knot, with the addition of tucking the

Improved Clinch Knot

free end upward into the top loop as shown. This extra loop is added for greater strength. Clinch knots are likely to fail if you tighten them by pulling on both the fly and the tag end of the tippet; only the tippet should be pulled. A singular disadvantage to the improved clinch knot, though a minor one, is that it uses more length of tippet, which means you will have to replace your tippet sooner if you make frequent changes.

Other knots used to connect the tippet to the fly include the surgeon's loop, the trilene knot, the palomar knot, and the simple figure-eight loop. The figure-eight and surgeon's loops are simple and can be readily tied on even small hooks. The trilene and palomar knots require passing the line through the hook eye twice, which may be impossible in smaller sizes.

Knot Treatment
Whatever type of knot you use, moistening the line will allow the two strands to slide over each other so that the knot may be drawn tight without excessively stretching and weakening the two materials. Saliva is an excellent lubricant. When you are tying streamside, be aware that even crystal-clear water may harbor bacteria that can cause severe illness, so avoid licking a knot tied with line that has been in the water. Moistening the knot with your dampened fingertips is safer.

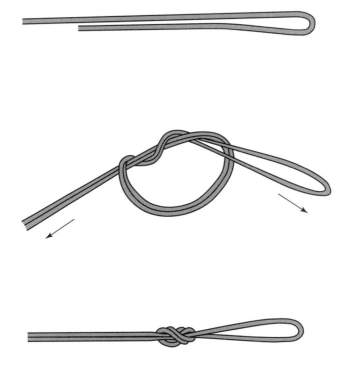

Surgeon's Loop

Knot treatments range from simple lubricants to adhesives. Flexible adhesives are a better choice, as they generally do not crack when the line flexes. Using brightly colored fingernail polish or typewriter correction fluid for knots in the first several feet of a leader will give you several markers in order to monitor drift and more readily detect strikes and drag. When combined with colored nylon, this method can be quite useful, especially when nymph fishing. A frustrating yet funny phenomenon is that some trout, especially recently released hatchery fish, will inevitably find your knots more appealing than your fly.

STRAIGHTENING LEADERS

Nylon will curl when wound around a spool. The ways used for straightening leaders are varied and usually rely on some combination of tension, friction, and heat. Numerous leader straightening devices have been sold over the years, most relying on the procedure of pulling the leader through

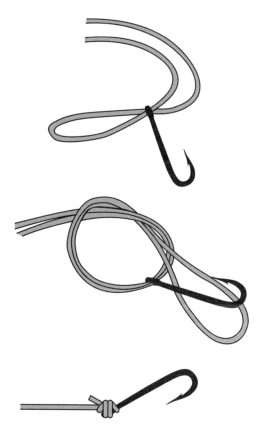

Palomar Knot

a closed layer of cloth, leather, goatskin, or even exotic dried mushrooms. The fatal flaw in all of these methods occurs when a piece of dirt becomes lodged in these materials. Nylon is softer than most soil particles, and it will become scored and weakened by continued scratching caused by repeated straightening. If you use a leader for only a few days, this is probably inconsequential. But if you use the same leader for weeks, the effect becomes significant. Nevertheless, I sometimes use a piece of chamois impregnated with silicone or fly floatant, which only proves that I do not fish often enough to wear out many leaders or that I change leaders frequently.

Gary Borger, in *Presentation,* provides a method of correcting memory (curling) in monofilament leaders. He recommends holding the two ends of the affected part of the leader between the thumbs and forefingers of

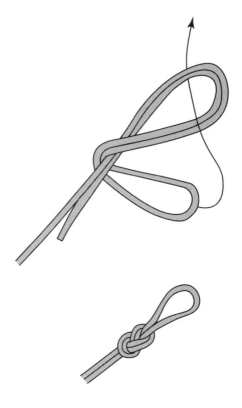

Figure-8 Loop

each hand and pulling them in opposite directions. Stop pulling just short of the point where the line slips in your grasp and hold it long enough to say: "Now you have a new memory." If this fails to straighten the section, it is likely that permanent damage has occurred and the segment should be replaced. Personal experimentation has led me to believe the incantation should be modified by the addition of a four-syllable term of your choice at the end; "woolly bugger" works well.

If the leader material becomes tightly curled by stretching or twisting during fishing, it may not be possible to straighten it. Permanent curling may result from excess tension on a softer monofilament, or it may indicate a leader that is too soft for the size of the fly, which is twisting either during casting or as it is retrieved. Molecular changes in the material may not be reversible by simple manipulation. Tight curls and spirals may indicate a need to replace part or all of a leader.

CHAPTER 6

Leader Designs

Before the advent of nylon, the limited length of gut segments limited the design of leaders. The same was probably true when leaders were made of horsehair. Now, with synthetic materials, the lengths and properties of the segments of a leader are varied, depending on the type of fly fishing. Leader formulas have been developed over the years to ideally present the specific types of flies used under the various combinations of environments the angler encounters. Separate designs have been formulated for small dry flies, wet flies, streamers, nymphs, and weighted nymphs. Other formulas have been developed for small spring creeks, larger rivers, windy conditions, and glass-slick water.

DRY-FLY AND DELICATE PRESENTATION LEADERS

Dry-fly and small-nymph leaders are designed to minimize the effects of drag and provide the most delicate presentation possible. The relative lengths of the three tapered components vary; however, the presentation taper, which includes the tippet, is the dominant and often defining section of the leader.

George Harvey designed his early leaders with the results of his experiment in mind. The ultimate goal of these leaders was to induce a series of S curves, rather than simply transfer energy to get the fly as far from the line as possible. Toward this end, he minimized the use of very stiff materials beyond the energy transfer section.

In recent years, Harvey has advocated the use of the most supple material available for all segments of the leader, tapering from a 0.015 inch butt to the desired tippet. A fairly constant progression from butt to tippet both in diameter (0.002 to 0.001 inch steps) and the length of segments (15 to 20 inch segments) results in a leader well-suited for delicate, low-drag applications. Lengthening the tippet adds additional S curves and diminishes drag.

Comparison of Old and New George Harvey-Style Leaders

Diameter (inches)	"Old"	Material	"New"	Material
0.015	20"	Hard Nylon	18" - 19"	
0.013	20"	Hard Nylon	18" - 19"	Softest Available Nylon
0.011	20"	Hard Nylon	18" - 19"	
0.009	12"	Soft Nylon	18" - 19"	
0.008	18"	Soft Nylon	15"	
0.007	22" - 28"	Soft Nylon	36"	
Total Length	**9.5 ft.**		**10.5 ft.**	

"Old" leader formula from *Techniques of Trout Fishing and Fly Fishing,* 1990. "New" leader formula from "Harvey's New Leader Formula," Fly Fisherman v.32, no. 6, Sept. 2001, and personal communication.

Lefty Kreh has also experimented with leader designs over the years, although he now concedes that he primarily uses store-bought leaders and finds them to be satisfactory. In contrast to George Harvey's design, Kreh, in his presentation at the Midwest Fly Fishing Show in Chicago in January 1999, stated that the stiffer butt section should be 50 percent of a leader. In his book *Presenting the Fly,* Kreh elaborates on his leader design criteria by stating that he believes the properties important in the butt section are weight and flexibility, as these relate to transmitting energy. Kreh's demonstrations of casting show that an expert caster can induce S curves using leaders with these criteria; however, some experts may be able to induce S curves casting with a garden hose, and, not all of us can cast like Lefty Kreh. And an examination of Harvey's leader recipe shows that 50 percent is stiff Maxima material, so the difference is basically a matter of definition.

While both men are world-traveled, George Harvey's style of leaders are likely to be based on experiences on his home waters, the spring creeks of Pennsylvania. These creeks can be fished with short casts, but the fish are often very selective, because the water is clear and shallow, and the fishing pressure is high. While Lefty Kreh's experiences are also varied, his preferences for leaders may be flavored by his experiences on waters where wind and the ability to cast for distance are as critical as being able to reduce drag.

There are some considerations when using leaders with as many segments as the Harvey type, most of them direct consequences of the knots. First and foremost is the necessity of tying all the knots. This is not an easy streamside task, so you should carry adequate replacements when using these leaders. Second is the tendency of knots to pick up dirt, algae, moss, and other vegetation from the water. The more knots, the more likely the

Vegetation or scum on the surface of the water can be a real headache when using knotted leaders.

leader is to pick up such material. The tendency of leader knots to pick up material may seem to be entirely disadvantageous, but there are times when this may be desirable, as it can help protect the fly from moss or other materials. It is easier to remove moss or debris that collects at the knotted unions in a leader than to pick this material out of a delicate fly. Third is the tendency of knots to increase the wind resistance of the leader, which slows it down during the cast. While this helps produce S curves, it also makes casting difficult in windy conditions and makes longer casts harder to control. It also ultimately limits the ability to use longer tippets, because the slower line speed will not allow longer tippets to turn over.

You should tailor your selection of leader design to the type of water you fish, your style of casting, and your level of expertise. If you cast with strong winds, Kreh's general ideas may make more sense, as they allow even moderately experienced casters to get the fly out there. If you are making short casts of less than 50 feet, particularly on water that has complex currents, Harvey's ideas may be more appropriate, as his leader designs almost force S curves into any cast.

BRAIDED LEADERS

Paul Burgess of Airflo patented the modern braided leader in the 1980s. Braided leaders are manufactured by weaving machines that produce a multistrand tapered leader with greater flexibility than conventional leaders without knots in the taper. As a consequence of their knotless construction and the suppleness of the material, they tend to cast smoothly and do not have a tendency to become wind knotted because there are no knots to hang up on each other. They will straighten out readily or form very regularly spaced and smooth S curves with the proper casting technique. Braided leaders do not tend to kink or develop memory problems, because they are made of relatively fine, supple materials.

There are some disadvantages to braided leaders, however. The braided leader has a hollow center, like a carnival finger cuff, that changes size as the leader flexes. This traps water in the core of the leader, which is expelled when the leader is picked up to cast, as the core closes when the leader is under tension. While water will flow through the weave of the leader, dirt may collect and build up in time. Casting spray is a difficult obstacle to overcome with these leaders, and on glass-slick water, it is considered a major problem. On streams with a fair amount of surface texture, such as riffles or pocket water, this factor is not a consideration, but the difficulty of mending these leaders complicates their use in fast-moving water. Their tendency to take on water and the added weight, plus their degree of suppleness, make braided leaders difficult to mend properly, lessening their suitability for wet flies or nymphs.

For those of us with less than perfect casting style, the point of the fly hook is prone to embed itself in the braid, causing sloppy splash landings at the very least, and tangled messes where barbed hooks dig into the weave. This tendency further keeps them from being the first choice when using more than one fly. Flotation is difficult to maintain with nylon braided leaders, as the leader already is denser than water and tends to take on

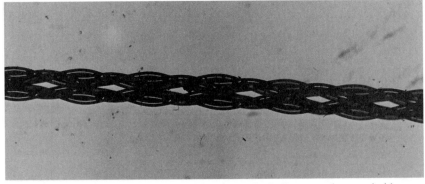

This microscopic photo of a braided leader shows the hollow core that can hold water in surface tension. The water may be released during false casting and can alarm fish.

water because of surface tension within the braid. They are not practical to make at home or streamside, and the cost is slightly higher than conventional leaders.

Braided leaders are well suited for fly fishermen who desire a leader that will turn over easily and straighten out. Given practice, you can develop the skills necessary to pinpoint cast these leaders into tight places such as overhangs, where very tight loop geometry is essential. Because braided leaders are supple, you can achieve tight loops with light lines and lower line speeds, allowing more delicate presentation. Combining a braided butt section with proper presentation section geometry will permit you to get proper turnover and dead-drift presentations on streams with moderately complex currents. Braided floating leaders are available, manufactured of materials that are less dense than water, and Airflo's braided leaders are treated with a coating and are woven tightly enough that spray is reduced.

FURLED OR TWINED LEADERS

The earliest reference to furled leaders is in the Charles Cotton version of Isaak Walton's *The Compleat Angler* (1676). Cotton depicts the "Walton's Engine," designed to prepare tapered leaders from multiple strands of horsehair. The method is similar to the manufacturing process used in twine or rope and has been adapted to modern leader materials. Makers of furled or twined leaders today loop a finer material back on itself in varying repetitions, and spiral twine it to form a tapered leader by twisting the material into a single strand. The procedure is described in detail in Darrel Martin's book *Micropatterns,* and simpler, less elegant devices than the finely machined Materlli equipment depicted in Martin's book can be made by anyone with the space and basic woodworking skills to do so.

To make a furled leader, two or three strands of prepared loops are spiraled in opposing directions, and the resulting fibers in turn are spiraled or intertwined to form a ropelike end product, held together by the tension of the opposing members. The thickness and therefore the stiffness of each portion of the leader are determined by the combined number of loops in the strands and the thickness and stiffness of the initial material used. The taper may be fine-tuned by altering the length and number of loops, so that when combined, the strands form a smoothly tapered leader. By winding the individual strands hundreds of times separately before combining them, then allowing them to unwind with each other in combination, they form a tightly furled line.

Furled leaders are knotless and will efficiently transmit the energy of the cast. These tapered leaders are limp enough to turn over with the slightest energy input, resulting in very straight-line presentations. With their streamlined taper and spiraled profile, they are less affected by wind than other knotted leaders. Their proponents claim that these leaders are less likely to pick up water, which can cause casting spray, or vegetation than braided leaders, but opinions vary. The weight distribution of the leader mimics the transition in a tapered fly line and has the same effect, aiding the leader in turning over. The furled surface allows line dressings for floating or sinking to adhere better than on single-strand monofilament. The furled surface also is not as prone to glare as a single strand of monofilament. Like braided leaders, furled leaders do not tend to have problems with kinking or memory, because they are made of thin, fine materials. The tightness of the twining reduces the chances of embedding a barbed hook in the leader.

Furled leaders also have some disadvantages. They are expensive, costing up to three times as much as a conventional leader, and they are more difficult to find premade. The manufacture of a 10-foot furled leader may take up to 50 yards of line. They also may weigh more than conventional leaders, because the energy transfer taper requires more material to be stiff enough to function efficiently, so if untreated, they may not float as readily as a knotless or knotted leader. However, if treated, they may float better than a braided leader, because they pick up less water and other foreign matter, which also helps in reducing casting spray. They are difficult to mend because they tend to be more supple and somewhat heavier than single-strand leaders. In general, they may not be as well suited for fishing fast-moving water because of line control problems during drift.

When using a furled leader, you may find that the weight compensates for the suppleness of the leader in aiding leader turnover. But the leader often straightens out too much for low-drag dry-fly presentation, unless you make adjustments in the cast, such as slowing the forward cast down to allow it to collapse or adding extra force to the forward cast and allowing the leader to recoil. Because furled leaders are difficult to mend, it is necessary to take measures to prevent drag before the line hits the water surface. The tendency to straighten out and extend to its maximum length can, however, be a desirable trait when distance is critical. The suppleness of these leaders and the resulting presentation may be best suited for lake or stillwater fishing with dry flies or smaller nymphs, where smooth turnover with delicate presentation is needed, but slack line is not necessarily as important.

SOME COMPARISONS
Braided and furled leaders are similar in that both are made of several strands of materials. The effect of having multiple strands is that the leaders are more flexible than monofilament leaders by virtue of the reduced

cross-sectional area. The total cross-sectional area of a braided or furled leader is less than that of an approximately equivalent monofilament leader because the air space between the individual round strands does not contribute to the total.

From a practical standpoint, the base material for a furled or braided leader may be anything, provided that it is within the range of thickness from 0.003 to 0.009 inch. The materials generally used for such leaders tend to be more flexible than standard monofilament line and include everything from silk to polypropylene thread. You should select the material based on the desired tippet, because the final leader may be made up of several strands of this material, woven or wound into a composite.

Both braided and furled leaders typically come in tapered designs. Stiffness is controlled by the cross-sectional area and number of strands. The stiffness in furled leaders is typically controlled by the number of strands of materials of relatively constant diameter. The thicker portions of the leader contain more strands, and the thinner portions are made up of fewer strands. Braided leaders may use individually tapered strands to achieve greater stiffness in the energy transfer section of the leader.

While the cross-sectional area of braided and furled leaders is less, the surface area of these leaders is greater than an equivalent monofilament leader. This affects the visibility of these leaders, as light is reflected and refracted by a larger surface area both above and below water. So either of these leaders will be more visible than a corresponding monofilament leader. In fact, braided and furled leaders appear almost opaque by comparison with monofilament leaders, especially fluorocarbon leaders.

Gary Borger states in *Presentation* that furled leaders, like braided leaders, collect dirt and algae. The greater surface area of these types of leaders provides more surfaces to attract dirt and algae. However, the degree to which furled leaders collect surface debris may be less than braided leaders by virtue of the tightness of the twining, resulting in less open area to trap small particles.

Furled leaders also differ from braided leaders in their twisting. Furled leaders are held together by the twining of twisted fibers. Braided leaders are held together by a weave of strands that does not produce twisting of the individual strands. When fibers break or become distorted, a braided leader may develop a kink or begin to unweave. Furled leaders have a tendency to curl over time, particularly if the twining is not exactly symmetrical. The twisting of multiple fibers in a furled leader results in a set of complex stresses such that the leader is in a constant state of torsion, which can be easily upset by the breaking or kinking of a single strand. The effect on a furled leader of losing a single strand is far more distortion than on a comparable braided leader.

Furled and braided leaders both tend to have a higher degree of stretch than monofilament leaders, so it may be possible to land larger fish without breaking them off. But if a multistrand leader is broken off when snagged on a tree or rock, you may be stung by the recoiling line.

LARGE NYMPH AND STREAMER LEADERS

Leaders to be used with large nymphs or streamers do not require the delicacy of a dry-fly presentation. These applications require a stiffer leader that can turn over the extra weight and maneuver wind-resistant flies during the cast. These leaders must also be capable of manipulating streamers or weighted nymphs underwater. And because the leaders are attached to heavier flies that are underwater, encountering rocks, snags, or the teeth of larger fish, these leaders should be capable of taking a little more abuse. All of these factors result in a leader design dominated by a stiffer energy transfer taper, with minimal transition and presentation tapers. Some heavily weighted nymphs and streamers may be cast and fished almost as easily with a level section of stiff monofilament as with a tapered leader because they are in effect catapulted in the cast, driven by the rod's response to their weight, rather than that of the line. But just as with dry-fly leaders, leaders for streamers and heavy weighted nymphs are sized by the line and fly size.

More critical than the taper for this kind of leader is the ability to get the fly where you want it. Assuming you want a weighted nymph or streamer to reach close to the bottom of a stream, the critical elements in this leader's design are the ability to turn the fly over without the collapse of the loop, which requires stiffer material, and the overall length, which determines whether the fly reaches the bottom. A rule of thumb that helps in this regard is that the leader length should equal at least twice the depth of the deepest water you are fishing, if there is a strong enough current to move the weighted fly. You can test this by trying it. If the fly stops on the bottom, shorten the leader. If the fly does not reach the bottom, you will not feel it skip along the bottom. You should first try mending line upstream during the drift, before considering lengthening the leader and/or adding weight.

The ability to manipulate the fly underwater does not imply that you can maneuver a streamer at the end of a 50-foot cast between rocks and obstacles, but the ability to strip line during a retrieve is fundamental to this type of fishing. If the leader is too fine for the fly, it will invariably twist, and when you go to cast, the first time the leader is out of tension, it will form the most atrocious mess imaginable. A stiffer leader will resist the tendency to twist, thus maintaining control of the fly during retrieve and remaining free of nightmarish rats' nests.

NYMPH AND WET-FLY LEADERS

Leaders designed for nymphs and wet flies fall somewhere between the extremes of the supple materials of a dry-fly leader and the stiffer materials of larger, heavier flies. Dave Whitlock advocates a leader for nymphs and midges that has an energy transfer taper of roughly 40 percent of the total length, a steeply tapered transition taper that is approximately 20 percent of the total length, and a presentation taper of roughly 40 percent of the total length. The energy transfer taper is sized to the line, and the tippet winds up at 0.006 inch (5X) material. This is somewhat finer than is needed for nymphs, and is probably better for smaller nymphs, but it is designed to allow its use both with nymphs fished anywhere in the water column and with midges fished at or near the surface. The whole formula for this 9.5-foot leader is as follows:

Dave Whitlock–Style Leader Formula

Section	Length (in.)	Diameter (in.)	Material
Energy transfer taper (stiff) 48 in.	24	0.018	Maxima
	12	0.016	Maxima
	12	0.014	Maxima
Transition taper (med. stiff) 24 in.	6	0.012	Maxima
	6	0.010	Maxima
	6	0.009	Maxima
	6	0.008	Maxima
Presentation taper (soft) 42 in.	6	0.007	Maxima
	36	0.006	Maxima/Climax

RIGHT-ANGLE LEADERS

Other leaders used for nymphs are designed to accommodate the use of both floats and weights. The designs that work best for this combination include at least one union that will deliberately hinge or bend abruptly, rather than transfer all of the energy of the cast. This is done to facilitate the sinking of the nymph and allow it to drift below the float. An example of this is the leader presented by Deke Meyer in an article in *Fly Fisherman* called "Right Angle Nymphing Leader." These effective leaders have an energy transfer section joined by a loop connection to a two-part vertical section that is both transition taper and presentation section. A float may be attached at the upper union. The energy transfer section is designed to be used with a floating line and works best when dressed to float as well.

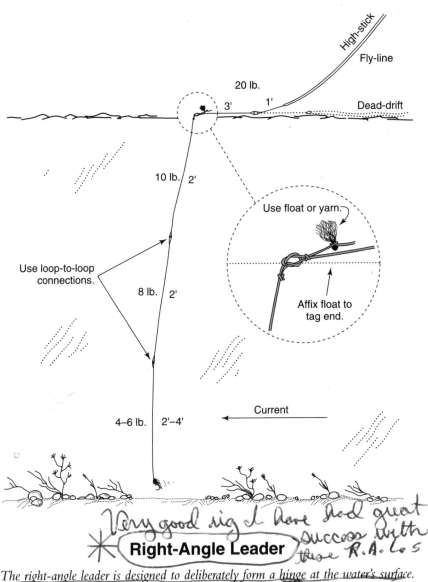

Fly-line

20 lb.

3' 1'

Dead-drift

10 lb. 2'

Use float or yarn.

Use loop-to-loop
connections.

8 lb. 2'

Affix float to
tag end.

Current

4–6 lb. 2'–4'

Very good rig I have had great success with these R.A.L.s

6"/9

✳ Right-Angle Leader

*The right-angle leader is designed to deliberately form a hinge at the water's surface.
It can be used with either "dead-drift" or "high-sticking" rod positions.*

Often a colored monofilament is used for the butt section to allow it to
function as a strike and drift indicator. The vertical section is designed to
hang below the float, with a BB-size split shot at the bottom. The tippet is a
24- to 36-inch section, with the diameter sized to the nymph at the bottom. Meyer's recommendation that the tippet be 24 to 36 inches long is
based on the belief that this length will allow a more natural drift; however,
shorter lengths from 12 to 24 inches will work as well in smaller streams and

are easier to cast, and longer lengths may be necessary in deeper or faster water, where a factor of 1.5 times the depth is a good rule to start with. The configuration is adjustable; make the vertical sections appropriate for the depth of water. The loop connections allow easy changes on length.

The right-angle leader uses connections that help force the leader to bend at the end of the butt section, accomplished by the loop connection as a hinge and the use of contrasting diameters of materials. The right angle and vertical alignment of the last two sections of the leader allow drift to occur such that the indicator is more directly above the drifting fly than with conventional arrays. This results in more immediate indication of a take or hang-up by the float. Loop connections allow substitutions of un-like materials, such as fluorocarbon and nylon, without so much concern for knot strength. Alternatively, a double overhand knot tied with the tag ends of the two components will force an acute angle into the leader and are just as fast to tie on the stream as making a loop connection.

John Judy devotes an entire chapter in *Slack Line Strategies for Fly Fishing* to what he calls a "Hinged Nymphing System," which is based on the same principles discussed above. He achieves the right angle in the leader by connecting the vertical section of the leader to the energy transfer section (which he calls the butt) with a clinch knot tied at a right angle, while the indicator (float) is tied to the tag end of the butt.

The vertical section is designed to be significantly thinner in diameter than the energy transfer section for two reasons. One is that by reducing the diameter, and thereby the surface area, the frictional drag on the vertical section is reduced. This reduces the bowing that commonly affects the drift of the fly and results in so much slack that more subtle takes and obstructions go undetected. The second reason is to abruptly change the energy transfer character of the leader, aiding in the hinging of the leader, a desired effect in this case.

The formulas developed by Deke Meyer are sized by line weight, a convention often followed by leader formulas, but not a prerequisite. The table provided in his article was based on pounds-test of the various segments and has been adjusted here to reflect diameters of nylon. The exact diameters are not as important as the relative thickness, since delicacy and precise loop control are not so much a factor with these leaders because they are used for fishing near the stream bottom. Judy uses the butt section of a knotless tapered leader that has been shortened by repeated alterations and might otherwise be discarded.

An essential element of fishing with a right angle or hinged leader is managing the fly line to maintain natural drift. On shorter casts, this can be accomplished by mending the line or by "high-sticking"—keeping most or all of the line off the water and following the drift with the tip of the rod.

To maintain a dead drift with longer casts, initial and frequent mends may be required to prevent a belly from developing in the line and dragging the fly downstream at an unnatural rate.

Right-Angle Nymph Leaders
(After Meyer, 1993)

Fly-Line Weight	Leader Segments Diameter (in.) Midsegments			
	Butt (48-in. length)	Upper (24-in. length)	Lower (24-in. length)	Tippet (24- to 36-in. length)
4 to 7	0.018 to 0.020	0.010 to 0.012	0.007 to 0.008	0.006 to 0.008
7	0.020	0.013 to 0.015	0.010 to 0.012	0.007 to 0.009
8 to 10	0.022	0.014 to 0.016	0.013 to 0.015	0.009 to 0.012

Notes: Adjustment of midsection lengths should be done by adding length to the upper segment. For fast current, midsection should be 1.5 to 2 × depth of water. For slow water, midsection should be 1.0 to 1.25 × depth of water. Line diameters reflect ranges for strength values given by Meyers.

MIDGE LEADERS

Leaders used for midges must be able to turn over the flies without any assistance from the weight of the fly, as with dry flies. They should be capable of allowing the lightest of flies to drift without excessive drag, because fish that are keying on small flies may also be paying greater attention to unnatural drift. In general, leaders used for delicate dry-fly presentation are suitable for midges, with the tippet sized for these smaller flies. Segments in the transition tapers may be longer, to allow a smoother transition to the tippet and because less energy is required to turn over the nearly weightless midges.

A couple fly-tying suppliers now carry larger-eyed midge hooks that will help in threading tippets. Another item that will help is a needle threader, available from sewing shops, or the fly-fishing equivalent, available for about three times as much from tackle manufacturers. At least one manufacturer markets fly boxes with threaders that can be preloaded with flies for easy on-stream use.

LEADERS FOR WEIGHTED LINES

Leaders used with sinking lines do not require a great deal of sophisticated design. The lines are dense enough that they pick up more momentum than conventional floating lines. This momentum is usually more than enough to turn over even the most bulky or heavily weighted fly, regardless of the leader. As weighted lines are generally used in either swift current (with resulting turbidity) or deep water (with limited visibility), the leader may be thicker and shorter than you would otherwise use. A leader of 6 feet made up of a 3-foot butt segment sized to the line and a 3-foot tip segment sized to the fly—or up to one size thicker for heavier-weighted flies—will perform well. A shorter, stiffer leader allows you to control the fly during drift or in retrieval and to feel the fly bumping along the bottom or when a fish takes it. It also reduces the likelihood of snagging the fly on the bottom or becoming wrapped up in submerged structure.

NIGHT OR LOW-LIGHT LEADERS

When fishing under low-light conditions or in turbid water, you can use heavier leaders without concern of detection. The potential for spooking fish is reduced by limited visibility, so the length may be shortened and the diameter increased accordingly. Such leaders allow more precise targeting of casts, and the stronger material also makes it easier to free snagged flies.

A formula of 30 inches–30 inches–30 inches, with the energy transfer section sized to the line, the presentation taper one size larger than the normal size for the fly used, and the transition section somewhere close to halfway between the two, will provide a good night stalker leader. The following are some suggestions for night-use leaders:

Night Stalker Leaders

Line Size	Fly Size	Energy Transfer (30") Diameter (in.)	Transition (30") Diameter (in.)	Presentation (30") Diameter (in.)
2-3	10-16	0.017	0.013	0.007
2-3	8-10	0.017	0.013	0.009
3-4	10-16	0.019	0.013	0.007
3-4	8-10	0.019	0.015	0.011
4-5	8-10	0.021	0.015	0.011
4-5	6-8	0.021	0.017	0.011
6-7	10-16	0.023	0.015	0.009
6-7	6-8	0.023	0.019	0.011

The presentation segment may be lengthened to get the fly to the depth desired, in the case of a nymph or streamer. Because these leaders are shorter even than most rods used, this formula will allow you to bring a fish in without worrying about snagging a large line-to-leader knot in the tip guide of your rod.

If possible, try casting such a leader a few times before you are in a low-light situation, so that you can make adjustments when you are still able to see. You may do this on the same water you plan to fish after dark to observe the way the line and leader behave, then rest the water for some time as darkness falls to allow the nocturnal predators to become confident of the safety of their surroundings. This will allow you to get the feel of the cast and see how far a cast will reach, how the fly lands and drifts, and where you may need to make alterations in your casting or in the leader to compensate for any problems. If you are lucky, you may catch a fish in the process. Although these leaders are strong enough to use to retrieve snagged flies, beware of the recoil. You are not likely to be wearing sunglasses at night, so unless you wear prescription glasses, your eyes will be at greater risk when pulling to retrieve a fly.

CONVEX-TAPERED LEADERS

Most tapered leaders have a relatively concave cross-sectional taper, with the taper thinning toward the tip. The rate at which the line thins is greatest at some point (the transition taper) before the tippet. An engineer named Bernard Beegle, believing that the same principles that apply to fly-line geometry should be used to design leaders, developed the convex-tapered leader in the early 1980s. The principle is simple: The energy transfer section of the leader is designed based on the conservation of momentum. To maintain loop speed, we should optimize the weight and speed of this part of the leader. Beegle's leaders look as though the energy transfer portion is simply reverse-tapered from a conventional Harvey-style leader, with a nontapered transition segment between this section and the presentation section.

Beegle presented three formulas in an article in *Fly Fisherman* in 1983, based primarily on the length of the leader. There does not appear to be any consideration to line weight in his discussion, and he tested the leaders

9 ft. 5X Convex Leader
(Beegle, 1982)

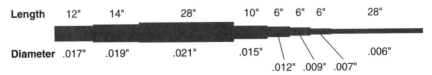

Schematic of a typical convex leader, showing proportions of segments.

without a line to verify their performance. The formulas are reproduced in the table below. After some experimentation, I modified the three formulas to more closely match line weights using the diameter-to-line-weight relationships presented earlier. The longer lengths are designed for intermediate line weights (5- and 6-weights) based on the assumption that a 5- or 6-weight rod is more likely to be used for a longer leader. You can modify these formulas for use with lighter rods.

Convex Leader Designs

Diameter (in.)	Length of segment (in.)					
	5X-9 ft. Beegle, 1982	6X-12 ft. Beegle, 1982	6X-15 ft. Beegle, 1982	5X-11 ft. for 5/6 wt. Kissane, 1999	5X-9 ft. for 3/4 wt. Kissane, 1999	6X-10 ft. for 4/5 wt. Kissane, 1999
0.017	12	16	18			12
0.019	14	24	32	14	12	14
0.021	28	32	40	18	24	24
0.023				30		
0.019					12	
0.017		14	20	12		14
0.015	10	10	16	8	12	12
0.013					12	
0.012	6	8	10	8		6
0.011						
0.009	6	6	8	8	6	6
0.007	6	6	8	8	6	6
0.006	26			28	24	
0.005		28	28			26

The convex or weight-forward configuration of these leaders makes them a particularly logical choice for windy conditions. Regardless of whether the convex geometry helps energy transfer, their ability to turn over well makes them useful for longer casts and larger flies. This is also a benefit when casting more than one fly.

It is particularly important to apply the simple energy transfer loop test to the first section of the energy transfer section and the end of the fly line with these leaders. Make sure the first segment of the leader is not too stiff for the line. Beegle's formulas are written using butt sections that may be better suited for lighter line (2- to 4-weight) based on the line-to-butt-section diameter criteria presented earlier; however, the stiffness of the butt section material will ultimately rule. The fact that the convex leaders are more specifically designed to transfer energy and continue the smooth loop movement from the line to the leader minimizes hinging potential even more here.

At least one line manufacturer has recently developed weight-forward knotless leaders. They are designed with the same notion presented by Beegle, but the commercial products are available as continuous-strand leaders, without knots. These weight-forward leaders are marketed as more efficient at turning flies over in windy conditions.

Provided the convex or weight-forward leaders are combined with presentation sections capable of producing adequate S curves to minimize drag, these may be the solutions to windy situations where turning flies over can be difficult.

KNOTLESS LEADERS

Some fly fishermen like knotless leaders because they are continuously tapered in the transition taper, which is desirable, and do not have knots to hang up on the fly or other knots if the loop crosses itself. They eliminate the need to tie many knots—a plus, especially at streamside. But as a whole, they may leave much to be desired.

This discussion will include only knotless leaders of a single strand of extruded monofilament rather than the more complex, but also knotless, braided, furled, and coaxial composite leaders. Without introducing technology that might make them cost prohibitive, it would be difficult to make a knotless leader from a single strand that would have variable flexibility through any mechanism other than its diameter. This is because different types or flexibilities of line may be used in a tied leader, but a single strand must rely on its diameter alone to vary flexibility. It would be difficult to find a material that would have both the stiffness necessary to make a good energy transfer taper and the suppleness for a delicate presentation taper within the range of diameters necessary for good taper geometry. So these leaders are typically somewhere between stiff and supple. Knotless tapered leaders are manufactured by an extrusion process that controls the diameter at specific points but is less precise in the geometry of the leader between these points. The various parts of the leader defined in this text in terms of diameter and function are not easily distinguishable in a knotless tapered leader, as diameter and consequently behavioral characteristics are continuously transitional, rather than potentially abrupt changes as with knots.

A close comparison of knotless to knotted leaders reveals that the transition taper of knotless leaders is longer and more gradual than most knotted leaders. This design characteristic compensates to some extent for the uniform stiffness. The length of taper varies from manufacturer to manufacturer and from type to type, such as bass versus trout leaders. The same length of taper in a knotted leader would result in a large number of knots, which are heavier and would result in more aerodynamic and water drag, to say nothing of taxing the patience of the person tying the knots.

A very annoying feature of these leaders is the lack of information provided by the makers. The typical labeling for knotless leaders identifies the tippet diameter, to an unknown degree of accuracy, as well as the overall length and maybe the type of use, such as simply "trout leader" or "bass leader." Often no other information is provided with regard to taper design, butt diameter, or relative stiffness. Yet all of these factors are as critical to the applicability of a leader as its tippet diameter and length. Without this information, the selection of knotless tapered leaders is very much a trial-and-error adventure. If you are able to talk off the record to manufacturers, you may find that there is quite a bit of variability in knotless leaders with the same designation from the same source. Manufacturing quality control is fairly accurate in setting the diameter of the butt and tippet sections, but the precision of the taper varies from batch to batch within a range that is acceptable to the manufacturer based on field tests.

Knotless leaders do have their uses, however. They are good introductory tools, as they are not as prone to developing wind knots as knotted leaders, so they are not as frustrating to the novice. And if you find a knotless tapered leader design that suits your needs, you can save yourself some knot-tying labor, provided the quality control in the extruding process is adequate to make a specific manufacturer's leaders behave consistently.

The best application for knotless tapered leaders may be to use part of them as a component of other leaders. If the knotless leader is particularly flexible, you can cut off its butt section and replace it with a more appropriate stiff material. If the knotless leader is particularly stiff, which seems to be less common, you can modify the tippet by adding an appropriate presentation taper. Either of these options will reduce the total number of knots. The process is likely to be somewhat trial-and-error, as the tapered sections of knotless leaders are typically much longer than the tapered portions of most tied leaders.

MULTIPLE-FLY LEADERS

In general, the leaders for multiple-fly fishing tend to be longer than those for single flies, and the tapers are somewhat different as well. Such leaders usually range from 12 to 25 feet, with the longer leaders typical in lake fishing. The flies may include a larger attractor as the first fly, followed by smaller wet flies or a wet fly and a nymph. The first flies are tied onto droppers that are perpendicular to the leader as the tags of a surgeon's or blood knot. The point fly is then tied on the end of the last tippet. The dropper and the end of the tippet onto which the point fly is tied are often one or two line sizes smaller than the preceding segment of the leader, but not necessarily. An alternative to droppers and point flies is to tie the successive segments to the bend in the hook of each fly with a clinch knot. If a large attractor (size 10 or larger) is used, the bend of the hook may be large enough to make this an easy matter; however, smaller lead flies are better connected to the tippets by splicing line onto the tag of the knot at the head of the lead fly.

Casting with Multiple Flies: The Scotch-Irish Way

Fly casting with multiple flies requires a different style from conventional single-fly methods. The fisherman with a single fly may include several false casts to get line into the air, to gradually increase line speed, or to dry out a fly. The Scottish or Irish fly fisherman cringes when he considers the problems such a method would cause on his waters. Imagine the tangles that can result from casting a three-fly array on a 20-foot leader into a stiff wind, then introducing false casts. It is not a pretty sight. But how to get the proper line speed and distance?

Scottish and Irish fishermen solve the need for line speed by applying a longer lever arm to the physics of the cast. Fishing from boats on open water or in the open country and manicured landscapes around their waters reduces the need for shorter rods and allows longer backcasts. Rods of up to 15 feet, twice the length of those used by many fishermen in the United States on small streams, are quite common on Irish and Scottish waters. The line speed at the tip of such a rod is considerably greater than that of even a 9-foot rod. The length of line to be used is first stripped off the reel and cast about 30 feet. Then, using the added leverage and radial speed generated by the longer rod, a single backcast is made with enough of a hesitation to load the rod. This allows the two or three flies to straighten out behind the caster so as not to wrap the leader around itself. Once the rod loads, the cast is brought forward in a single power stroke. Single or double hauling (pulling line in as the rod flexes to add load and increase line speed) can be used, although these methods are not common among traditionalists, whose casting style appears far more relaxed and graceful than the typical American techniques.

Although tapered leaders are more efficient for casting, the leaders used for Irish lough (lake) fishing tend to be simple step-down tapers of only a few segments, based on the water clarity or the size of fish anticipated. The point fly sections are knotted to the leader (called a "cast" in Ireland and the United Kingdom) with either surgeon's or blood knots. This method is used almost exclusively for wet flies and nymphs, as dry flies are not as commonly used on lakes in Ireland. The high winds in Ireland and Scotland make it necessary for fishermen to cast almost exclusively with the wind, which compensates somewhat for the inefficiency of the simplified leader geometry.

SPECIALTY COMPONENTS
Shock Tippets

The term shock tippet is often used to describe the addition of a stronger or more abrasion-resistant material to the presentation section of a leader. The shock tippet is designed to prevent fish or abrasion from reef rock or boulders from cutting the tippet material. If fish are the problem, the shock tippet need only be placed where the fish are likely to cut the material, about the last foot or so. If the problem is abrasion by rocks or reefs, the tip section may need to be 2 or 3 feet.

Shock Gum Sections

Shock gum sections are elastic segments added by some fly fishermen to prevent fine tippets from breaking off fish. You can place the section any-where in the leader, but it should not cause a high contrast in the flexibility of the materials, as a hinge may result. Thus you need to determine the flexibility of the shock gum material relative to the other components of the leader.

Shock gum sections will protect a fine leader tippet from breakage if a large fish makes a sudden run. The elasticity of the material may hinder the ability to set the hook in some cases, and it is particularly important to use sharp hooks. Such segments can cause greater recoil if the fly is snagged; exercise caution when attempting to free a snagged fly, and be prepared to duck.

Colored Leaders

You can use pigmented monofilament material for any part of the leader, but it is usually limited to the heavier segments of the leader. A colored segment or segments in the energy transfer section act as a built-in strike detector without impairing the cast or requiring bobber. The color also makes it easier to see if drag is developing in your leader. The most com-mon material for this purpose is a running line called Amnesia, available in either red or chartreuse in several different strengths. By using a micro-meter or comparing the line stiffness to the Amnesia line, you can select an appropriate match to the fly line. If you choose to use two colors, you can track the drift of the two colored sections relative to each other, further enabling you to see the effects of drag and detect subtle strikes. Several manufacturers have incorporated fluorescent butt sections into their knotless leaders for the same purpose.

Color can be used as a camouflaging feature as well as a strike or drag indicator. Leader materials are typically available in either clear monofilament or dull olive or brown colors. Natural colors in a trout's environment tend to be irregular in their distribution, rather than occurring at abrupt intervals, as would be the case with the segments of a leader. If absolute stealth is required, particularly in the subsurface, you can easily add olive, tan, gray, and black to your leader with waterproof felt-tip pens, allowing ten minutes or so for the colors to dry before using the leader. Pens in these colors allow quick streamside modification of fly patterns as well and are useful additions to your fly vest.

There have been several articles on the use of white or silver coloring in the presentation section of the leader when fishing caddis nymphs, as some species are known to spin a fine thread. Coloring the last foot or so, particularly the length between the nymph and split shot, if used, is said to be a reasonable simulation of this phenomenon. The split shot is probably inconspicuous enough, and the white or silver tippet looks like the anchoring thread of the nymph.

Weighted Sinking Leaders and Lines
Commercially available sinking heads provide a means of getting a nymph or streamer to the bottom, even with a floating line. They typically consist of a braided or composite section of lead-core line or similar material that is connected to the leader either at the line or within the thicker portion of the leader (the energy transfer section). These sections are heavy enough that they are difficult to cast smoothly with anything less than a 5-weight rod, but they make it possible to fish a deep-water pattern in moving water without adding additional split shot to the tip or having to resort to a different line. The weight of the sinking-tip section determines the rate of descent through the water column. These weighted segments are usually fitted with loops at both ends and serve well as the butt section of the leader.

Leaders that incorporate a sinking tip should be designed similarly to those designed for use with a sinking-tip fly line. Attaching a one- or two-segment tippet with a total length of no more than 5 or 6 feet (with the final segment sized by the fly) to the sinking tip works best. Longer leaders allow the fly to be whipped about by the current and may result in an unnatural drift (at least) or in the leader becoming snagged on bottom structure (at worst). Because the fly is being fished on the bottom, the leader does not need to turn over in a gentle, elegant arc, so the leader or tippet design need not be very sophisticated.

When deciding whether to use a weighted fly, split shot, weighted or sinking leader, or sinking line to get the fly down in the water column, the way the fly will behave as a consequence of the weight is important. Most near-bottom flies are partially fished using some kind of retrieve or action imparted to the fly. During a retrieve, the path the fly follows along the bottom of the stream varies with the method chosen.

A weighted fly on a floating line and neutral-density, monofilament nylon leader is picked up nearly vertically off the bottom and bounces in a series of hops determined by the length and quickness of the stripping. The floating line will buoy a moderately weighted nymph, such that it will drift by bouncing along the bottom, simulating the natural. To add a level of activity, you can slowly strip in line with hesitation, allowing the fly to rise up along a nearly vertical ascent; then, when you hesitate, it will drop back to the bottom. You can do this to simulate a retreating crayfish, with quick retrieval stripping using strips of 3 to 6 inches. A similar pattern of strip and retrieve, but with much smaller strips, say an inch or so, works to simulate the movement of scuds or freshwater shrimp. You can simulate small, bottom-feeding baitfish with this combination of movements, as well as relatively mobile nymphs prone to bouncing off the bottom, such as stonefly nymphs. A nymph used with a split shot will wiggle at the end of the tippet as if anchored to the bottom by the weight. When you strip the line, the nymph will follow the bouncing course of the weight but will stay above the bottom of the streambed.

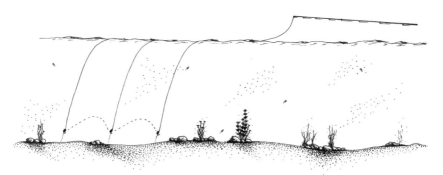

Retrieval of a weighted fly with a floating leader results in a slightly inclined ascent. By interrupting the retrieval and allowing the fly to drop, you can achieve a bouncing trajectory.

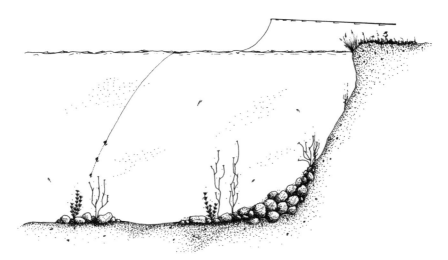

Retrieval of a weighted fly on a sinking-tip line results in a moderately inclined ascent.

A second combination involves the use of weight on the fly, but with a sinking-tip fly line. With a floating line and a sinking or weighted leader, the fly will rise at a roughly 45-degree trajectory off the bottom and pulse back downward as the retrieve hesitates. A steady stripping retrieve with this arrangement pulls the fly up in a gradually angled ascent, much like a natural nymph in its ascent to the emerger stage. You can modify this arrangement with a hesitation, allowing the fly to drop back to the bottom, and can also use it to simulate retreating crustaceans, such as crayfish or shrimp.

A third combination involves a weighted nymph and a sinking line or a heavily weighted sinking leader butt. Retrieval will keep the fly moving along the bottom with minimal ascent. Slowly crawling crayfish, bottom-browsing minnows, or any creature that remains essentially on the bottom

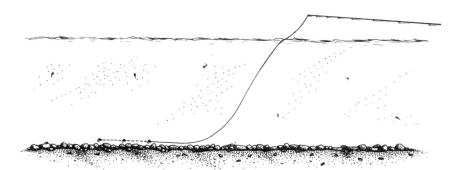

Retrieval of a weighted fly on a sinking line results in the fly moving along the bottom, simulating a creature that remains on the bottom.

can be simulated with this combination. This method may be best suited for some types of fly fishing, but the fly, leader, and line may become tangled on any angular projections on the bottom. This can be a particular nuisance in turbulent water with submerged stumps or sweepers, or where large boulders are present. Not only is there a high risk of losing the fly and part of the leader to snags, but there is also a real possibility that the line and leader will be weakened by abrasion when dragged across submerged boulders. When this arrangement is used in lakes, or where the bottom has a significant amount of silt and clay, the dragging of an over-weighted line or lead weights may stir up clouds of silt, further decreasing the chances of success. To avoid this, keep the line from dragging on the bottom for great lengths of time.

CHAPTER 7

Rules of Thumb
and Leader Myths

LEADER DIAMETERS

The labeled diameters of leader materials are not always accurate or precise. Accuracy here refers to whether the measurement is correct. Precision refers to the relative size of the units used in stating the dimension; a measurement in thousandths of an inch is more precise than one that rounds to the nearest hundredth of an inch.

The inconsistency of accuracy may be due in part to inconsistent conversion from metric units used in the countries where the materials are manufactured to decimal fractions of an inch. A comparison of five different materials all labeled as 5X (0.006 inch) revealed a variability of ±0.0015 inch from one manufacturer to another. I made the measurements with a caliper micrometer calibrated to 0.001 inch and checked the data against an English unit printed micrometer microscope grid and a microscope. I took five measurements for each material and recorded the mean value. None of the materials measured had a mean variation in diameter of more than 0.0005 inch, which indicates a reasonable degree of consistency.

Labeled vs. Actual Diameters of Leader Materials

Name	Labeled Diameter (in.)	Labeled Strength (lb.)	Mean Measured Diameter (in.)
Dai Riki Velvet	5X (0.006)	4.40	0.0062
Dai Riki Fenwick	5X (0.006)	4.75	0.0056
World Class	5X (0.006)	4.50	0.0063
Maxima	5X (0.006)	3.00	0.0068
Cortland	5X (0.006)	4.90	0.0056

As the true diameter and the labeled diameter often differ, care is required in preparing leaders. Several manufacturers are improving the level of accuracy and precision in leader and tippet diameter information, even to the extent that they report the diameter to four places to the right of the decimal point. Still, if you are preparing leaders and the person who developed the formula you are using just went by labeled diameters, you may have difficulty duplicating the leaders without knowing whether the design was based on measured or labeled diameters.

A good friend, Clint Pedersen, whose interest in leaders in no small part inspired me to begin the research that resulted in this book, tells me he uses a micrometer to measure each new spool of line used in leaders and marks the spool with the correct diameter before using it. While you are marking the diameter of the line, you should also write the date of purchase on the spool to keep track of its relative age.

Individual manufacturers tend to be consistent, so that a manufacturer's 4X will be larger in diameter than its 5X. Many authors suggest staying with one brand of material throughout the leader. In practice, it may only be necessary to stay consistent for each functional section of the leader. This recommendation is based on the implied consistency of physical properties of the nylon and how this may affect knot strength and ease of tying. But it may also be good advice based on the tendency for one manufacturer to be at least consistent in diameter labeling, if not entirely accurate.

The importance of diameter is related to the influence it has on the stiffness of the material. Having a high level of confidence in the consistency of all material properties, but especially diameter, is important in minimizing the repetition of field mechanical tests to evaluate each segment of a leader during construction. As you become a better caster, you may learn to adjust your casting style to compensate for a leader that behaves differently than expected. But you may not get a second chance to make a perfect cast to a particularly spooky fish, so it is best not to have to go through trial-and-error on the stream.

LEADER MATERIAL STRENGTH

Manufacturers have listed the breaking strength of their leader materials for years, and they are almost without exception conservative. This may be in part due to their not wanting to disappoint the consumer who expects the leader to hold up under the load of the biggest fish he will catch. But there is a pretty wide range of values for both nylon and fluorocarbon materials.

Leader and Tippet Material Breaking Strengths (BS)
(Reported in Pounds on Packaging and Catalog Listings)

Breaking Strengths

Diameter (in.)	.003	.004	.005	.006	.007	.008	.009	.010	.011	.012	.013	.014	.015	.016	.017	.018	.019	.020	.021	.022	.023
Size	8X	7X	6X	5X	4X	3X	2X	1X	0X												
Mason								4	5	6	7				12		16		20		
Maxima Chameleon	1		2	3-4	4	5	6	8	10	10	12		15		20		20				
Cortland 333		2.1	3.3	4.5	6	7	8														
Cortland Tipmaster II	1.5	2.2	3.2	4.9	6.2	8.2	10	13	14												
Cortland Fluorocarbon Tipmaster				2	4	6	8		10												
Climax II		2.5	3.5	5.5	6.5	8.4	9.5	12	15		17		20		28		35		42		
Climax Super Hard						2.5			6	10		12	15				20				
Fenwick Leader Class		2	3	4.5	6	8	10	12	14.5												
Rio Powerflex	1.5	2.2	3.2	4.9	6.4	8.2	10	13	15												
Scientific Angler Mastery Series		2	3	4	5	6	7	9	10												
Amnesia a/	1.5													15			20			25	
Maxima Clear	1.5	2.3	3.2	4	4.9	5.7	6.6	8	10		12		15		20			25		30	
Dai Riki		2.4	3.5	4.75	6	8.25	11	13	15		19		15		30		36		44		46
Dai Riki Velvet			1.75	2.4	3.75	7.25															
Dai Riki Diver Fluorocarbon				3.5	4	5	6	8	10												
Umpqua		2	3	4	6	8	10	12	14												
Orvis Super Strong	1.75	2.5	3.5	4.75	6	8.5	11.5	13.5	15.5	18.5	20		25		35		40		50		60

a/: Measured diameter, diameter not listed on packaging

Note: Data from catalogs, packaging, and advertisements collected from 1995 to 2000

THE RULE OF FOURS

The "rule of fours" is a widely held notion that you can determine the tippet size for a leader by dividing the hook size by four. This implies that a #12 fly is best managed with a 3X tippet, and a #20 fly by a 5X tippet. Most modern fly fishermen use finer tippets than 5X for midges in the #20 range, and 5X or 4X tippets are commonly used for sparsely dressed dry flies in #12 through #16. Though the "rule of fours" may be a good starting point, it does not take into account the variability of fly patterns. The energy transfer section and the transition taper play the greatest role in turning the fly over. The size of the tippet should be adjusted for the bushiness of the pattern, the weight of the fly, the taper of the leader, the wind conditions, and the typical length of cast.

THE TWO-STEP MYTH

For years it has been preached that the taper in a leader should decrease by increments of 0.002 inch or less. Gary Borger conducted a series of experiments with leaders to determine whether larger differences in diameter would cause hinging. He concluded in his book *Presentation* that diameters could differ by as much as 35 percent, which translates to a difference of approximately 60 percent in cross-sectional area, without significant hinging. Based on this observation, he adjusted the Harvey-type leader formulas to reduce the number of knots by increasing the steepness of the taper.

The two-step theory falls apart entirely when going from the line to the leader. Fly lines are typically made of a finer supple Dacron or similar core material, coated by a lightweight polymer plastic, usually polyvinyl chloride but sometimes polyurethane. The two-step principal is not appropriate for a connection between two materials with such high potential difference in stiffness as nylon or fluorocarbon and a polymer-Dacron composite.

THE MYTH OF THE GENERAL-PURPOSE LEADER

Several authors have presented the notion of a general-purpose leader. Lefty Kreh advocates a leader that starts out with a stiff butt section and is tapered down in steps by halving the length of each successive section until reaching the tippet, which may be anything from $1\frac{1}{2}$ to 4 feet. He suggests starting with 4 to 5 feet of stiffer material and ending with a tippet length dependent on the application and need for unencumbered drift. This rough formula will result in a leader that will cast well and turn over smoothly; however, if you do not also consider the stiffness of the materials in the taper, the leader may not produce the S curves necessary for low-drag drifts. A highly skilled caster can adjust his cast even during an initial false cast if he detects something in the behavior of a leader that requires adjustment. But the average fisherman will probably make several casts before realizing a problem exists.

Gary Borger has designed what he calls the Uni Leader for general-purpose use. In *Presentation,* he explains how to modify the two end sections to accommodate different conditions, so it is really not a single leader, but a well-designed series of leaders based on the somewhat fixed transition taper, adjusted at either end to suit the conditions.

A large variety of over-the-counter leaders are available today, both knotted and knotless. The greatest problem with many of these products is the lack of information given to the consumer. The leaders are typically labeled as to the tippet size and the length, with little or no additional information as to the taper or design. The characteristics of each section of the leader determine whether it will work with or against your type of fishing. Even if the manufacturers provide the tippet and butt section diameters, you still do not know the overall properties of stiffness and the relative lengths of the tapered sections. Some manufacturers have started labeling their leaders with more information as to taper and the type of fishing the leader is designed for, and it is possible through trial-and-error to find over-the-counter leaders that are appropriate for specific conditions.

There can be no such thing as a general-purpose leader, because there are too many variables. You can fish with any type of leader that will fit through the eye of a hook, and you can certainly catch fish with mismatched leaders, but the selection of a leader that is tailored to the application will add to the ease of casting and will likely add to your success.

CHAPTER 8

Leader Adjustments and Modifications

SECTION OR TAPER LENGTH ADJUSTMENTS

When fly fishing exploded in popularity in the United States in the early 1990s, some sporting goods stores sold leaders based on rod length, because, after all, you would not want your leader to get hung up on the guides. Even expert writers on the subject occasionally implied that the length of the rod was an important consideration in selecting the length of leader. If the leader used was too long, the butt section would be kinked at the tip-top, where the leader would be bent during transportation, as the tension imparted by the line with a fly in the hookkeeper pulled it tight. If the leader used was too short, it would be ineffective at deceiving the fish or hiding the presence of the larger fly line. However, the length of the rod should be a trivial concern in establishing the length of the leader. Leader length should be based on the length of your average casts, the line weight, wind conditions, and whether you need long, low-drag drifts or are fishing in deep water with sinking flies. Transportation considerations should not have any bearing on the proper design of a leader. If you feel the need to draw your leader tight when you move from one location to another, you will have to deal with the potential curling or kinking of the leader when you get to your next position. This is better than selecting your leader length based on rod length.

The segment lengths in leader recipes used today probably continue to reflect measurements used in the days of natural materials, when lengths were limited by the source, such as horsehair or catgut. Although synthetic fibers can come in any length, some recipes still use segments of similar lengths to those of yesteryear. Perhaps as the last of the fly fishermen who grew up casting gut leaders pass their rods on to their grandchildren, these traditional limitations will be put to rest, and design can be based on performance alone.

Individual casting style and ability have great bearing on the need to fine-tune leaders. A gifted caster may be able to perform well with a single leader for a multitude of fishing requirements. If you find that you can compensate for a leader's shortcoming without inconveniencing yourself or twisting your arms like a contortionist, do so. It is much more enjoyable to fish than it is to tie blood knots. If, on the other hand, your casting appears to be ineffective, determine what aspect of the cast or leader is causing the problem and, if necessary, make adjustments accordingly.

If you are casting less than 30 feet, your leader will make up about one-third of the total line-and-leader length in a cast, a smaller proportion if you are shooting any line (although the need for shooting line at 30 feet is rare). As a consequence, leaders for short casts should have shorter components, in essence becoming miniatures of lines for average, 30- to 50-foot casts. The exception is the presentation section. If you are using short casts, it is likely because you are on smaller waters or casting in similar close conditions. The need to minimize drag on spring creeks is critical, as is the need to maintain stealth. So the presentation section should remain as long for short casts as for long casts. If you are fishing on a glassy spring creek with no wind and a small dry fly, you should consider a leader, including tippet, of 10 feet as a minimum. You may want to adjust the tippet for drift and the energy transfer section for wind.

If you are fishing under low-light conditions with a lighter line, a 5-weight or less, on rough water, you may be able to use a shorter leader, between 7 and 9 feet. A lighter line has less impact on the water as it lands, so the concern for stealth is not as critical as with heavier lines. The consideration for stealth remains critical on slick water. When using a shorter leader, you can adjust the tippet length to obtain the correct drift. You may want to adjust the energy transfer section to compensate for increases in wind speed.

If you are fishing a medium-size nymph, #10 to #14, in water that is 8 feet deep, you should consider using a leader with enough softer or finer material in the transition and presentation tapers to allow the nymph to sink to the bottom. Such a leader might be over 12 feet long (one and a half times the depth), depending on the speed of the current, as the leader will not be straight up and down, so it will require greater length to reach the bottom. The old notion of fishing nymphs on tight lines cast down and across has been modified, and upstream-cast, low-drag drifts for nymphs are now as common as they are for dry flies. So you may want to use softer transition and presentation tapers than might be recommended in older recipes for nymphing.

In general, you can size the overall length of the leader based on application, then adjust it as you observe its performance. If you observe that fish appear to be spooked by the line as it hits the water, and you cannot attribute this phenomenon to your casting limitations alone, you can lengthen the leader. Lengthening the energy transfer taper alone may cause the line to straighten out and induce drag, and if the fish are spooked by fly line, drag will likely cause them to flee as well. So it is best to consider adding length to the tippet first to reduce the potential for alarming fish. If additional material is still needed, then you may adjust the transition taper.

There are two methods of length adjustment you can make if a leader straightens out too much. From an energy standpoint, the initial response may be to shorten the energy transfer section, thereby shortening the overall length and slowing the line speed. But this may cause a greater risk of spooking fish with the line. As an alternative, you may want to lengthen the leader if you see it straighten out too much for your purposes, in the event you desire a low-drag drift. If you add length to add S curves, you generally should add length in the last two segments of the presentation taper.

Another consideration is that of line slap. This occurs when the line hits the water at a high speed, because of either an exaggerated follow-through in the cast or too much line speed. Sometimes casting adjustments alone can remedy line slap, but adjustments in the length of the presentation section can also slow the speed of the fly enough that it lands more gently on the water at the end of a leader full of slack. Using a 12- or 14-foot leader on a medium-size stream is not unusual, but it is all too often overlooked as a strategy on small streams, and this is where the conditions may most warrant it. The effects of line slap are reduced by longer leaders. If you have to cast from a more distant spot to get enough line out to use a longer leader, that distance may be just the thing needed to keep your presence from alarming spooky fish.

Some fisherman use tippet sections a foot longer than recipes specify to give them enough extra tippet to have surplus when they change flies. They may change a fly after a couple of fish demolish it, maybe even a couple of changes go by, and then they notice that the fish seem to stop hitting. It is very possible that the extra foot was giving them a gentler, more drag-free drift, and when they shortened it, even though they were still within the recipe, the change was enough to add drag that resulted in the fish's sudden lack of interest.

Although anglers seldom take the opportunity to examine the line in great detail as it goes through the cast and lands, there are times when this is possible, either from your vantage point or through the eyes of an observer. If hinging is occurring or the size of the S curves in the leader as it hits the water is not satisfactory, you may have to adjust the transition taper of the leader. This may be done by adding sections intermediate to those in the taper or by replacing suspect segments with longer lengths of the same material. The unions in the leader itself may help add some S curves, so it is not always necessary to replace a segment; you may only need to add another length of the same material.

COMBINING MATERIALS

The notion that leaders should be made with a single type of material has been around for years. For the most part, this has been the result of experiences where unlike materials proved difficult to knot together or one material actually cut through another in tightening the knots, as one material was significantly harder. Some experts have advised keeping materials the same throughout the leader because their experience was that the leader performed more consistently if they did.

But rather than blindly following this rule of thumb, it may be preferable to understand where it applies and where it can be broken. The possibility of unlike materials forming weak unions due to one cutting the other is valid but may be exaggerated. If the knot is properly lubricated before tightening and is tightened gradually, one material may be less prone to cut through the other. Slicker or harder materials may not hold together well because of lower friction in the knot, but a knot dressing that includes an adhesive may help minimize this problem. Still, there may be cases where two materials are incompatible. Trial-and-error experimentation is sometimes necessary. Make a test knot, wet it thoroughly, and pull on it gradually until the line breaks. It is essential to wet the knot, as it will be wet when used. If the knot fails, consider going back to using like materials; if the knot holds and the line breaks elsewhere, you can assume the materials are compatible.

Some materials may not perform well together because of significant differences in stiffness. Consider the case of a fisherman following a recipe he has used for years based on one type of line. He runs out of that manufacturer's 2X and substitutes another 2X. He checks the knots and, finding them sound, believes he has found a suitable replacement. When he casts, he notices that the loop collapses when it hits the new material. A knot results, and he has to stop fishing to untie it. Even though the new material was the same reported diameter as his old reliable line, it is less stiff, so the transfer of energy is inefficient at the knot. It is also possible that a hinge has developed.

A second example with the same circumstances will illustrate what can happen when a stiffer substitute material is used. In this case, the loop opens up when it reaches the new material, and as it does, the loop and fly are caught by the wind and hang up in brush overhanging the stream. Had this not happened, the loop may have collapsed when it moved from the new material to the softer older material toward the tippet, as the contrast between these materials may have been great enough to cause a hinge.

In the examples given, the materials could be different brands of nylon. What would happen if one of the materials was fluorocarbon? The diameter of the material is not the only control on the suitability of the material. The overall performance resulting from its stiffness and its weight determines whether it will perform well or not. If you check the fluorocarbon material for stiffness and place it in the leader at an appropriate location in the taper, joined by sound knots, it should work well. The use of such a combination of materials may be ideal for nymphs or emergers, where you want the fly to hang below the surface as it drifts. The additional weight of the fluorocarbon material may be just the thing you need.

DESIGN CHANGES

Sometimes you may find a leader formula that you like for one application, but you cannot leave well enough alone. Other times you find the leader you used at the start of the day no longer performs well because of a change in wind or the flies you are using. For whatever reason, you need to have some idea how to modify the leader that will result in a positive outcome. If you want to alter the leader in midstream, rather than change the whole leader, you may want to consider changing segment lengths or substituting a different material for one or more segments. Some general guidelines can be helpful, but individual experience will ultimately prove what modifications suit you best.

Changing Segment Lengths

If you move to a part of the water where casting greater distances or greater stealth is required, you may need to adjust the energy transfer segment of the leader. Lengthening the segments in the energy transfer segment alone may be sufficient for longer casts. But if control of a longer leader is difficult for you, you can extend the energy transfer function into the transition taper by lengthening the first segment of the taper—the thickest—by 3 to 12 inches, without losing too much control. Other than this modification, it is generally best to leave this section of the leader alone.

There are a few instances, other than nymph fishing, where a short, less than 7-foot, leader is preferred. Nymph leaders differ so much from dry-fly leaders that changing the whole leader may be preferable to changing segments. If you have to make very close casts where you need the control that is provided by the fly line, but want to be delicate, a shortened dry-fly leader may be the tool you need. If you are troubled by wind, shortening the overall length of the leader may seem to help you control the cast, but it is likely that you are sacrificing presentation for what you believe to be better control. Still, you can shorten a leader while bearing in mind that a leader that is shorter but has more S curves in it is likely to be more effective than a longer leader that straightens out too much. So you should not shorten the presentation section in the interest of keeping the length manageable. If shortening the leader seems to be necessary, take the length from the energy transfer section.

Adjusting the length of the presentation section of a leader is an easy way to add slack to your presentation. It is also necessary as the tippet becomes shorter from changing and replacing lost flies. If the tippet section breaks off but is still more than 12 inches, you can splice another section to it, even using the same-diameter tippet material. The knot between the two materials will form one location for a bend in the leader that will add slack, and the length will add to the ability to form S curves. Just be sure the knot is sound and the end it is tied to is not damaged by whatever caused it to become shorter.

Maintaining the same relative stiffness of materials while making these modifications is usually a good idea. Changing more than one variable at a time during an experiment, while it may achieve the desired result, does not always allow you to determine which variable was more critical. So while you change lengths of segments, try to keep materials constant. If that does not seem to be the key, then consider changing the material itself.

Substituting Materials

If you are using a nylon monofilament, you can change the character of a leader greatly by substituting fluorocarbon segments. Fluorocarbon is less stiff than monofilament, but its weight is greater. So the energy efficiency may not suffer too much, as the momentum of the loop is maintained by the additional weight of the material, rather than the stiffness. You can, then, add suppleness to the leader by substituting fluorocarbon segments. The finest tippet materials are usually soft enough that this is not a problem, and you may be able to put enough pop at the end of your cast to prevent problems if you realize the potential ahead of time.

But once you go from nylon to fluorocarbon, you should not go back, except maybe at the tippet. Some fluorocarbon is so much softer than corresponding diameters of nylon that the fluorocarbon will not transfer energy to a succeeding segment of stiffer nylon. Conservation of momentum (mass times velocity) works in theory, but it is difficult to maintain casting loops when the velocity changes up and down in response to changes in the mass of the leader, and the end of the cast may fail to even turn over.

The guidelines presented here can be summarized by some basic observations. Dry-fly and dead-drift presentations are improved by leaders that form S curves when cast. These S curves act as shock absorbers to reduce the effects of drag. If the S curves are not forming, and you cannot adjust your casting style, consider lengthening the presentation taper.

Adjusting the presentation section of a leader in consideration of wind can be done in a number of ways. If you are casting predominantly downwind, a longer, finer tippet can provide excellent presentation with nice S curves for a dry fly. A stiffer or heavier segment slightly longer than a lighter one called for in the recipe can be just as effective if wind has added enough chop to the water's surface to conceal a larger-diameter material. And if the fish are particularly large or energetic, a longer, yet stronger segment may be a better choice anyway. A stiffer tippet can help when casting into a stiffer wind; however, casting downwind with a stiffer tippet can result in the leader slapping the water and spooking fish. It is not practical to change tippets every time the wind or your casts change direction, but you should adjust the speed of your forward cast to compensate.

If the leader is not turning over, consider shortening the presentation taper or using a finer tippet. If you do not want to shorten the presentation segment, you can try a couple of other alternatives. You can increase the energy of the last part of your cast. This may provide enough energy to proceed through the loop and turn the tippet over. Another option is to increase the efficiency or stiffness of the energy transfer section of the leader by either changing the material, which is not always possible, or shortening the segments in it, because the effective stiffness is inversely proportional to the length of the segments.

If you do not feel comfortable adjusting the leader or dropping the tippet size to a finer diameter because of the need for strength, fighting wind, or distance, you can try adding knots as a means of inducing the line to form slack S curves. But this, too, can effectively weaken the leader if the knots are not tied properly or tightened sufficiently. Even the best knot may not be as strong as the unspliced line.

Nymph and wet-fly leaders should be tapered to allow accurate casting and allow the type of drift or swing desired. You may adjust the length of the presentation taper to determine the depth of drift. As with the dry-fly leader, you can adjust the energy transfer taper to achieve greater casting distance or control of the fly during casting and drift.

Streamers and heavy-weighted nymphs are difficult to cast and require thicker, less flexible leaders. Materials that are too flexible will not only fail to turn over, but will twist as the fly is cast or stripped.

Leaders for night or low-light situations should be designed so that you have confidence in your control. You often cannot see well enough to evaluate problems in these cases, so it is best to experiment before light conditions become severe. Keep the low-light leader relatively short and strong, as you may need it to hold up in retrieving a snagged fly.

A skilled caster can cast a poorly designed leader very well. An unskilled caster may cast a well-designed leader very poorly. But the chances of success are greater with the right leader, because the drift that occurs after even a poor cast may have less drag.

CHAPTER 9

Paraphernalia

Fly fishermen are gadget collectors. Lee Wulff is credited with the invention of the fly vest sometime in the 1930s. But it wasn't until the press corps photographers during World War II demonstrated the utility of similar vests, and traded them with GIs for everything from souvenirs to photo opportunities, that the fly-fishing vest became an essential part of our attire. Since that time, we have been trying to see how much stuff we can put in the thing. A sample of almost every item ever put in the fly fisherman's vest has been lost in swift or deep water, so you should attach a simple line or a springed retractor to anything you cannot do without, or that would be considered an inappropriate addition to a trout's living-room furnishings.

TOOLS

Only a few things are necessary to make leaders: leader material, a means to cut it, and most importantly, the patience and dexterity to tie the necessary knots. Knot-tying gadgets are available that may or may not make life more bearable, and the devices available for cutting leader materials range from your teeth (not recommended by my dentist) to gold-handled scissors (a costly item, especially if dropped into a fast-moving stream). A cheap pair of nail clippers is more than adequate but has the distinct disadvantage of being a high-visibility item by virtue of its chrome plating. Diehard do-it-yourselfers can come up with any number of ways of relieving these things of their glare, but the fly-fishing versions, with their matte finish, are not that expensive and don't require you to turn your kitchen sink into a deplating chamber to remove the chrome finish. But either of these options will also suffice in trimming your nails, if they are long enough to be a problem when tying knots. Knot-tying guides or diagrams are useful for those of us who were never in the navy or do not have the time to

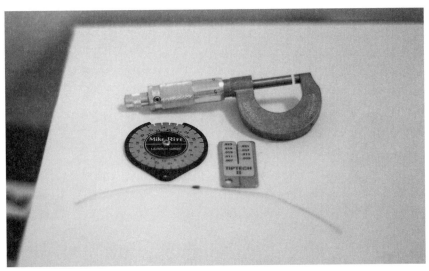

Measuring devices for leaders and tippets.

memorize all the knots we need to know. You can make or purchase knot cards; they should be a convenient size and waterproofed or laminated.

A micrometer is a useful item to have if you are serious about this whole affair. But if you do not want to invest in a good one, the measurements on leader material spools are close approximations, and the relative sizes of materials of the same brand are at least a consistent guide when making leaders. A good-quality micrometer is not a piece of field equipment, as it may become damaged or lose its accuracy. The nearly disposable notched discs available for leader tying are not as accurate, but they are not so expensive that you would be heartbroken by their loss or damage in the field.

PORTABLE LEADER KITS AND WALLETS

Fly fishermen use kits for fly tying, and leader tying is simpler, so the kit should be too. A durable box or nylon bag that will house the necessary materials and tools will suffice. You have to decide what to carry in the kit and what to carry in your vest. The container should be water resistant, so that it will withstand a certain amount of inclement weather, and light-tight, so that ultraviolet light will not deteriorate nylon monofilament. Store the container at room temperature or in a cool, dry place when not in use, to preserve the materials in it to the greatest extent possible.

Unless it is a financial hardship, the kit should be capable of standing alone without components having been temporarily transferred to your vest. This means that spools of materials in the kit can be larger capacity if you do a lot of fishing, and buying these materials in quantity may save you money. Include spools of your favorite manufacturer's lines for all the sizes

The author's homemade leader book.

of leaders you use or are likely to use. This means a range from approximately 0.025 inch to 0.005 inch (6 X) or 0.004 inch (7X) diameter. Use a waterproof marker to mark the purchase date on each spool so you will not wind up tying a dozen leaders with monofilament that is too old. The kit should include a clipper, a bottle of knot dressing, a bottle of cyanoacrylate glue, a few bottles of colored fingernail polish for strike or drag indicators, and a notebook or card for formulas. An excellent alternative to the conventional fingernail clipper is a pair of cuticle clippers, available at most drugstores. I find cuticle clippers better for cutting off tag ends of knots because they have a smaller, pointed tip, allowing you to clip the tags off right at the knot. You should have a micrometer or at least a notch gauge, even if you believe the manufacturer's measurements. A 6-foot folding carpenter's rule is the best thing I have found for measuring lengths, as it is compact and the hinges provide a place to tuck the line you are measuring. You might include a very small retractable tape as a backup. You may also want to keep a selection of strike indicator materials, such as foam and yarn, in your kit so that someone going through your vest will not find them there and question your ethics.

Leader wallets have been around for years, too. Many are well made of composition materials, with a variety of options for storing your leaders. So far, my favorite idea for a leader wallet is a small, vinyl looseleaf notebook that can be fitted with reusable Ziploc bags as pages. The notebooks are available at stationery supply stores in a variety of sizes. The best size is determined by the size of your vest pockets. Ziploc bags come in a variety of sizes, but it may take a little searching to find a size to match the note-book. After placing a strip of duct tape along one side as reinforcement, punch holes in the bags to fit over the rings in the binder. You can label the bag with waterproof, color-coded markers or use stick-on labels, which have a tendency to detach themselves. For added organization, you can insert file page separators to divide leaders by type, such as dry-fly, nymph, and wet-fly. Because they are inexpensive and thin, you can use a separate bag for each leader, avoiding tangles.

In your vest, in addition to the leader wallet, keep another clipper, a smaller inventory of spools of leader tippet materials, and a few sizes of thicker monofilament. Carry a size range consistent with the type of fish-ing you expect to be doing, about six or eight spools. Leader dressings for sinking and floating the line and a small vial of knot dressing are also nice to have, and because most vests have far more pockets than anyone can fill, there is probably room.

VISUAL AIDS
Many people find that the close nature of leader-tying work requires addi-tional magnification, and the cheapest way to achieve this is through simple magnification reading glasses, available at most pharmacies for less than $25. These may not be handy at streamside, but a pair of half glasses in the vest pocket might be just the thing you need.

LEADER DRESSINGS
Two types of line dressings may be used for leaders: those for adjusting the leader's ability to float or sink, and those used to strengthen the knots. The use of line treatments keeps you from having to change lines to make them float or sink under intermediate conditions. There have been some envi-ronmental concerns regarding the potential effects of various line dressings on water quality, especially when some products seem to spread an oily film on the water. Several companies now market environmentally friendly products that are either biodegradable or do not contain compounds that are damaging to the environment. Consult product labeling.

FLOATANTS
Numerous floatants are available, including sprays, pastes, powders, and waxes. Nothing can make line any lighter than it already is; these products act to keep the line from breaking the surface tension of the water and keep things floating. Most floatants are marketed for use on flies but may be used equally well on line or leaders. The sprays tend to be

uneconomical, as the volume of the containers is largely occupied by the propellant, usually propane. Applying a wide spray to a thin line is a wasteful practice. Waxes or pastes, usually silicone based, are easy to apply and tend to stay on the leader for a reasonable duration without needing frequent reapplication. Older references, like Bergman's *Trout,* contain recipes for dressings that are just plain dangerous, but they come from a time when applying a mixture of gasoline and paraffin to the line with your fingers was not seen as a dangerous practice, and the effects of such things on the environment were not widely known.

LINE SINK

There are probably as many different sinking agents available as floatants. These products tend to be surfactants that reduce the surface tension to allow the line to sink. A simple weak detergent solution, applied with a wet cloth or chamois, will achieve the same result. Another solution is the surfactant used in photography called Photo-Flo, which is inexpensive and easily applied. Using stream mud will also work by roughing up the surface of the line and lowering the surface tension, but it will shorten the life span of your leader or line by abrading the surface and increasing the tendency for dirt and algae to accumulate. Some fishermen moisten their fingertips with the slime from the first fish they catch and use it to dress the leader so it will sink. Though this works, your fingers may damage or contaminate the fish's slime layer, making the fish susceptible to lethal fungus and bacterial infections. Additives used to sink flies or leaders, which are already heavier than water, are more difficult to counteract than floatants, so take care in their application.

FLOATS

Although the use of floats is controversial, they are here to stay. Floats come in all shapes, sizes, and materials. The most common include small foam discs with adhesive backing to attach to the line, polypropylene yarn that is tied onto the leader, or any number of clever attachments of plastic or wood. Some even use the old red-and-white plastic bobbers favored by bait fishermen, perhaps in direct defiance to traditionalists. One upscale manufacturer, in an effort to make our lives easier, sells polypropylene yarn floats precut to a specified size, fitted with a fine wire loop to attach to the leader. Some of these devices must look strikingly similar to some food in the trout's diet, as they are often struck at with more vigor than any attractor pattern.

These floats are multi-purpose, in spite of the term strike indicator. The most common use of the float is to detect strikes, surely enough. But although the float may appear to be only going along for the ride, it does affect the travel of the fly. Most commonly used in connection with the nymph, the float will keep the leader between it and the fly in tension, because it is usually placed close enough to the fly that little slack develops—otherwise, it would not detect subtle strikes. By maintaining tension between the float and the fly, the float pulls the fly off the bottom from time to time when water deepens, thereby acting as a means of keeping the fly from stopping in its drift.

You an assess the degree to which drag has affected the drift of the fly by following the travel of the line, the float, and the water around it. If the line and float seem to be traveling at a flow rate markedly different from that of the surrounding water, possibly indicated by the drift of stream debris or insects, drag is occurring. If you are concerned that drag has damaged the presentation, you can adjust the placement of the float, change the length of the leader, modify your casting technique to throw more slack into the cast, or mend the line once it is on the water.

SINKERS OR WEIGHTS

Lead has been a part of fishing for as long as anyone can remember, but its time may be nearing an end. Concern for the potential introduction of lead into the environment has led to its being banned in most, if not all, U.S. national parks, and many states are considering similar regulations. Modern-day weights are made of tungsten and other synthetics.

Weights on the leader can help get the fly to the desired depth. A few tricks can help reduce the risk of problems. Pinching a split shot onto the leader can cause a kink or a weak spot. You can avoid this by tying a stub of line onto the tippet and attaching the split shot to it. For heavier weights, you can reduce the potential for losing your fly to bottom snagging by tying on a piece of thin rubber band as a stub and pinching the split shot to it. If the weight hangs up, it either springs free or breaks off without taking the fly with it.

Strip lead has been around for quite some time, and the same type of weighting material is now available in nonlead material. This type of weight is not as secure as split shot, but it allows you to put exactly the amount of weight you want on the leader. The same is true for the newer weighted putties. Check such weights from time to time to make sure they are still secure. You can control slippage by placing the weight materials between knots.

CHAPTER 10

Casting and Fishing Techniques to Minimize Drag

The following paragraphs describe some common casting techniques that help fight drag. Too many fly fishermen begin false casting and laying out casts before they have any idea what the trout may be feeding on, what current lanes exist, or even whether there may be any fish in the area. Unless you already know the water, take a few moments to look around you. After you choose a fly, decide if your position is the best possible one from which to present it. If you can better your position, do so carefully. If you cannot, consider carefully a casting and mending strategy.

The principle technique in minimizing drag is the introduction of slack line and S curves into the leader so that the line and leader can move in response to the currents with minimal effect on the drift of the fly. The key is learning to get the longest possible drift before drag occurs and, if possible, adding slack during the drift to prolong the effective length of dead drift. You can read volumes of books on the subject of casting, and you can watch hours of videos, but there is no way to master the techniques other than casting on moving water. If it has been a while since you have been fishing, you may want to find an unlikely stretch of water, where you can warm up and not spook fish in the process, before hitting the more promising areas.

GENERAL CASTING TECHNIQUES

Casting instructions commonly refer to arm positions using the hour hands of a clock. The forward horizontal position of the rod is 9 o'clock, directly overhead is 12 o'clock, and straight back behind you is 3 o'clock. The conventional overhead cast traditionally has been based on movement of the rod between 10 o'clock and 2 o'clock, with a stationary elbow. This casting technique was derived using very flexible cane rods with heavy lines that loaded the rods deep into the thicker portion. Modern equipment and faster composition rods have resulted in higher line speeds, and the range of conventional overhead casts is now closer to 10:30 to 1:30.

Common errors in casting include using the arm motions for throwing, that is, applying excessive shoulder movement, follow-through, or wrist snap. A traditional teaching trick is to have a student hold a book under his casting arm to force him to keep his elbow at his side during the cast. An Irish gillie took this a step further with me while fishing on a windy lough in County Galway. He asked which of my fly boxes had my best flies in it. After I told him, he put the box in my right armpit, briskly tucked my elbow to my side, and said, "There, now hold that there while you cast. Maybe that'll provide some incentive for you to do it right. Remember, you're no' throwing a bloody baseball." This little trick forces the caster to cast with the elbow rather than the shoulder. An athlete who is used to throwing a ball using his whole upper body will tend to resist this style, but it works remarkably well, and a skilled fly caster can cast just as far in this manner as one who insists on using every muscle above his waist.

The follow-through (letting the forward cast progress beyond 10 o'clock) is a particularly bad habit and will almost always result in the fly line hitting the water well before the fly, alerting the fish to something unnatural in its environment. An exception to this is using wrist snap to provide enough energy to turn over a longer leader on short casts. Although intuition may lead you to believe a follow-through will add distance to a cast by lengthening the distance the rod travels, it will not. The additional travel by the rod is less than one foot with a 9-foot rod, and this travel occurs largely after the line has started to make contact with the water or, at the very least, is on its way downward rather than forward.

In contrast to the follow-through, a backward drift of the rod after a brief hesitation at the backcast can actually add to the loading of the rod in the forward cast and lengthen the distance of the cast. The backward drift is done after the elbow has stopped flexing by rotating the shoulder backward while keeping the elevation of the hand constant. It should be done without dropping the rod tip, so the line stays high and the loop does not cross itself. This move adds some distance without ruining presentation like a follow-through.

A wrist snap can have the same effect on a cast as it does a baseball, imparting a twist, or a quick acceleration. If not done precisely, it can also force the rod to descend below 10 o'clock and have no good effect at all. Doug Swisher and George Harvey advocate a wrist snap at the end of the cast to add line speed and to fine-tune the presentation. But this is something that should only be added after mastering the conventional cast, as it can result in bad habits that are hard to break.

Holding the butt of the rod in the cuff of a jacket sleeve can help prevent too much wrist snap in casting.

A trick that traditional casting instructors use to prevent excessive wrist snap requires students to wear long sleeve shirts or jackets. The cuff of the casting arm is pulled toward the hand and the butt of the rod is tucked into the cuff of the shirt, forcing the wrist to be cocked somewhat downward at the start of the cast. The cuff keeps the rod butt from pivoting, thereby preventing the wrist from flexing upward. This also forces the caster to hold the rod at the top of the cork, which provides more accuracy and control. Commercial wrist braces are now marketed in fly shops for the same purpose.

THE DISADVANTAGES OF DISTANCE CASTING

Distance casters are wonderful to watch. A full line arcing across the horizon in majestic loops is the image most people associate with fly fishing. But great distances are seldom rewarded with great fish. Most fish are caught within 50 feet of the caster. And the longer your cast, the more water comes in contact with the line, so the more your fly will drag. Another disadvantage of long casts is the difficulty in mending. A third problem, assuming you beat the first two or the trout fail to recognize that you have not, is setting the hook. Often you have so much slack in the line that any but the most extreme hook set is ineffective. And even if you are able to set the hook, the time required to do so may allow the trout to spit out your fly. In fact, long distance casters may not even realize how many strikes they get, and even with strike indicators or floats, the reaction time is too great to overcome.

LINE WEIGHT AND CASTING

Fly-line weights are based on the first 30 feet of line, as this was once thought of as the typical length of aerialized line in a cast. Longer casts are now commonplace, and this convention is outdated, but it has been maintained for the sake of consistency. For rods designed with modern materials and tapers, the proper loading of a rod may not be achieved with a cast less than 30 feet, if the line used is matched to the manufacturer's designation, because many line tapers are skewed, with the lightest section at the tip. Some authors suggest using one line weight heavier if you expect to use predominantly shorter casts. This may make the casting mechanics more balanced and get the rod properly loaded, but if you are casting short distances, you need greater stealth, which will not be provided by a heavier line. An alternative is to overpower or accelerate your casting stroke on shorter casts, resulting in a loading similar to that in a 30-foot or longer cast. This way you will still have the stealth of a lighter line and will not have to change spools as often. In fact, you may find that for 3-weight and lighter rods, a line that is one weight less than the manufacturer's rating may produce a far gentler presentation—what we normally seek with lightweight rods anyway—when cast with a little extra acceleration. Another advantage of overpowering the cast is the rebound that occurs at the end of the cast, as in the bounce cast.

THE BOUNCE CAST, OR TUCK CAST

The bounce cast is characterized by the abrupt termination of the forward casting stroke, causing the rod tip to bounce and recoiling the line and leader somewhat. The result is a series of S curves that tend, when all conditions are right, to decrease in size toward the tippet and fly. The cast can be achieved in a number of ways and can be combined with other techniques as well.

The easiest way to execute a bounce cast is to modify your forward cast stroke so that it accelerates continuously from the backcast until your arm reaches about 12 o'clock, where you suddenly stop all movement. It is similar to shooting line, except that you are not releasing line at the end of the forward cast. Once the loop moves forward from your rod tip and the line straightens out, but before the complete recoil, slowly lower the rod tip and allow the line to settle onto the water. If you are shooting line in the cast for extra distance, you can simply and abruptly stop the line with a finger on your line hand, and the same recoil should follow.

A second means of imparting the bounce at the end of the cast is to pull back just slightly on the forward cast just before the loop straightens out, then follow the line downward with the rod tip.

This cast has also been called the tuck cast because, when executed with sufficient crispness, the leader will actually tuck back on itself at the end. This is particularly beneficial when casting nymphs upstream, as it allows the fly to descend in the water column before being pulled downstream by drag.

THE CURVE CAST

The curve cast is achieved by introducing a sidearm component to the forward cast. If the cast is executed by a right-handed caster with the arm at the three-quarter sidearm position, the line will curve to the left. A mirror-image cast by a leftie will result in a curve to the right.

You can induce a curve in the line by executing a bounce cast in the horizontal plane, as the line will tuck horizontally as readily as vertically. You can also combine the two casts to get a series of S curves after some practice.

A curve cast has several applications, both in fighting drag and getting your fly to a desired target. The curve cast was probably developed to get flies into tight areas of overhanging brush or downed trees while keeping your line from snarling such obstructions. Be prepared to direct any fish away from the obstacles immediately upon setting the hook. Introducing a curve upstream will add slack line to your drift, and introducing a curve and S curves lengthens the dead drift even more.

THE REACH CAST

Like the curve cast, the reach cast creates a curve in the line as it lands on the water, which acts to counter drag. You execute this cast like a standard overhead cast, completing the forward cast with an initial stoppage of the arm at approximately 1 o'clock, but sweeping the arm left or right in an arc from the elbow, keeping the wrist stiff, just as the line settles to the surface. This arc is transferred to the line, which lands with the corresponding curve. It is almost as if you are painting a curve in the line as it falls. If there is little wind, you can watch the curve follow your rod tip, with the arc convex to the right when you sweep to the left. To achieve a curve that is convex to the left, simply sweep your arm to the right at the end of the cast. This cast is effective in tight spots that might make mending difficult or where mending after the line hits the water might spook wary fish. You can combine it with the bounce cast or curve cast to increase the effect.

THE WIGGLE CAST

The wiggle cast, also called the S cast by some, is another way of adding S curves to the line and leader. This cast involves the simple side-to-side wiggling of the rod tip just as the loop straightens out. The greater the energy imparted to the wiggle, the larger the S curves.

The wiggle cast requires that you develop control of the rod beyond the simple movements of a conventional cast. All of this sounds rather simple, and it seems that anyone should be able to achieve this, even to the point that you could tailor the size of the S curves from the fly to the line, increasing in size toward the tip of the rod. In theory, all of this is possible. But practice differs greatly from theory, and you may find that timing the wiggling with the descent of the line and leader is not nearly as simple as it sounds. With practice, this technique can be added to other casts, thereby increasing its utility.

THE ROLL CAST

Roll casting is useful in close quarters or where there is limited room for a backcast. Lay a length of line and leader on the water as straight as possible. Pick up the rod tip so the line leaves the water but the leader and fly stay on the surface. Send the first length of line out with a flip. Then pull back at a rate fast enough to load (flex) the rod but not fast enough to pull the fly or leader off the water. The fly and the leader thus anchor the cast as the rod is loaded.

In a conventional cast, the line forms an overhead loop. In a roll cast, the line forms a D loop, where the rod is the straight stem of the D and the line arcing backward forms the curved part. Once the D has formed, the rod begins to load because of the resistance of the anchor. The roll cast is executed with a continuous stroke because a hesitation between the backcast and forward cast allows the tension needed for loading to dissipate.

The arm movement for a forward roll cast is virtually identical to that of a conventional cast, the arm stopping at the 11 or 10 o'clock position. Roll casting differs from conventional overhead casting largely in the mechanism for loading the rod. Conventional casting depends on the inertia of the line and the acceleration of the backcast to load the rod, whereas roll casting relies primarily on friction and surface tension between the leader/fly and the water. (It is this aspect that makes roll casting difficult to practice without water, because dragging a leader and fly through grass is not a very good simulation.)

You add distance in roll casting by shooting more and more line during forward casts. This is best done at an angle away from your target, preferably upstream some distance, to avoid startling the fish. For the same reason, the retrieve and backcast should begin after the line is well past the area you're fishing. And if you miss a strike, resist the temptation to start another cast immediately; you'll almost certainly spook the fish, and you probably have too much slack in the line from trying to set the hook.

A common problem stems from leaving too much line on the water's surface during the backcast. The wake from the line is tremendous and will startle most fish in the area. The ideal backcast leaves only the leader and the fly on the surface, reducing, though not eliminating, the disturbance.

The leader must be straight at the beginning of the backcast so it creates enough surface tension to load the rod. Larger flies or weighted flies offer greater resistance to retrieval, so the need for friction and surface tension between the leader and the water is somewhat reduced, and a shorter leader may be used when roll casting such flies. "Long" and "short" are relative terms, of course, and leader length is determined by several factors. But for a weighted size 12 nymph, you might start with a 9-foot leader, and for a weighted size 8 nymph, with one as short as 7½ or 8 feet. A leader that is too long will absorb too much energy in loading to make a good roll cast with a larger, heavier fly. No matter how straight it is at the start of the backcast, if your leader is too long, your arm will be at the back of the loading position before the rod is flexed enough to execute the cast. Also, the heavier the fly, the stiffer the energy transfer section should be in order to turn the fly over properly. A soft leader will not form or maintain the right loop shape during the cast to transmit the energy necessary.

A longer leader is needed to roll cast a small fly effectively because the fly itself exerts little resistance to backcasting and is essentially no help in loading the rod. So a size 16 Adams or a size 18 Pheasant Tail Nymph may require a 10- or 12-foot leader.

ADDING LINE TO THE DRIFT

Line can be added in a couple ways to lengthen the distance that a fly will travel with minimal drag. It is essential that S curves or slack line be maintained in the leader, as once the slack in the leader is gone, drag has control of the fly. If the leader is straight, your best bet is to convert your presentation to a wet-fly swing or a dry-fly surface skip or, if you are not close enough to a trout that might move to take the fly, pick up and recast. If, on the other hand, there is still slack in the leader but your line is losing its S curves, you can add line and even restore S curves to the line. The simplest way to do this is to strip line from the reel and feed it out through the guides, but you should do this in a way that adds S curves while not disturbing the fly in its drift. Adding line while raising and wiggling the tip so that the line, but *not* the leader, picks up off the surface allows you to add both line and S curves. This technique cannot be mastered without practice.

A second method is to feed line off the reel into the line hand and insert an abbreviated roll cast into the line, stopping short of a full rolling loop, feeding enough line into the cast that you do not straighten the leader. Ideally, your roll cast should not be "felt" by the leader, but only add line to the drift. This method requires that your line be on the water, as the rod is loaded by the surface tension for roll casting. When you see the line losing slack and want to add line, strip 10 feet or more of line from the reel, depending on how much you wish to add to the drift, and keep it in the hand not holding the rod. Raise the rod tip as though to make a conventional roll cast, but rather than pulling line backward as you normally would to load for a roll cast, allow the line to come from your free hand as you raise the rod. Then flip the roll cast forward, continuing to let line from the free hand feed into it rather than pulling line from the water into the casting loop. Stop the forward cast abruptly to form slack S curves.

PRACTICE, PRACTICE, PRACTICE

Not even a library full of books or videos can substitute for field practice. Find a stream or body of water where you can cast, even if no fish are present. Ideally, the body of water will have a varied flow, allowing you to try casting in several different scenarios, but even if it is no more than a still pond, you can practice casting and line-handling techniques. Strive first to create S curves in the line and leader, then work on controlling the size or number of these curves. Try to use the same rod and line you will use on the stream, and alter the leaders as you would under real conditions. Use a fly or a small piece of yarn that you can see when it is cast, and follow its movements and presentation. Avoid large hunks of yarn, as they have greater wind resistance than most flies and will not respond as a fly would, possibly causing you to develop bad habits.

Repetition of casting techniques will result in your ability to perform various casts without much thought or analysis. Try to make the same cast to the same spot ten times in a row. When you succeed, try a different cast but the same target. Watch the way the line behaves with different casts, and watch the fly to see which casts result in less drag or a more natural presentation. Try combining casts in different ways. When something works, repeat it again and again, and do not stop until you can repeat the results consistently without a second thought. Then alternate casts with each other. This will allow you to develop the skills necessary to cast well under a variety of circumstances.

Practice with different wind conditions too. Wind can be a friend or foe in fly fishing, and you cannot control it. You can sometimes control your position with respect to wind, but this is not always the case. In time, you can develop casting skills that will allow you to reach fish with casts into the wind or away from it, minimize drag in your drifts, and be able to add extra feet to the distance your fly will drift before drag pulls it in an unnatural course.

FISHING A TIGHT LINE

"Tight lines" is a common salutation among fishermen, but it does not mean we always want the line to be tight when there is no fish on the other end. Still, there are times when this is desired. Fishing streamers, nymphs, wet flies, or dapping dry flies are just some of the times when we want to have control of the line, and control equates to a tight or relatively slack-free connection from the fly to our hands.

A major consideration when fishing a tight line is how to conduct the retrieve. There are several options, presented below. Something to consider for all of these methods is the effect the rod has on the retrieve. If you retrieve the line with the rod at an angle to the current, so that the rod flexes, it will damp out any variation in the retrieve and eliminate any pulsing and all but lengthy hesitations. This may be a desired effect, as with something like an upstream-swimming baitfish, but you usually want some hesitation. So retrieves are almost always best performed with the rod pointed toward the fly. This also allows a more direct feel of the take, and if you remember to set the hook with a sideways rod movement <u>and</u> a tug of the line with your line hand, you will have better success.

The Wet-Fly Swing, the Leisenring Lift, and the San Juan Shuffle

The classic wet-fly swing was developed over one hundred years ago to present a pair or trio of flies on a long leader and line. You typically make this cast diagonally to the current in the downstream direction, allowing the array of flies to swing under tension until it stops directly downstream of you. Many fishermen experience a high proportion of strikes when the flies are directly downstream of them, and this has been attributed over the years to a number of possible causes. One of the most likely is that the fish have followed the potential meal around in its drift, and as it drags and rises in the water column, they want to check it out to see if it is really food before it disappears. A fly rising in the water column at the end of the drift in what has come to be known as the Leisenring Lift behaves similarly to an emerger shedding its wings and approaching the surface. Most wet flies already have their wings out, but trout are only so smart, and even though what they see may look like one kind of food but behave like another, they may assume the fly actually is some kind of food and take a chance.

There is a second, less savory, possibility. Fish tend to line up downstream of fishermen, particularly where scuds or other rich foods are present. The fishermen unknowingly (unless they are truly dishonorable) dislodge these creatures from the undergrowth, and they float downstream on the current to the waiting gluttons. The deliberate practice, known as the San Juan Shuffle, named for the San Juan River, is now illegal in many locations. Nonetheless, it is responsible for large numbers of fish being caught every year, whether intentional or not. The trout get so used to feeding on whatever bounty the currents send their way that a wet fly, a nymph, or even a dry fly may just seem like an appetizer.

Downstream Dry Flies

Fishing a dry fly upstream was once heralded as the only "proper" way to fly-fish. If you locate a trout feeding at the surface and can present a reasonable representation of a fly in a dead drift, odds are pretty good you will at least get a strike. But downstream dry-fly presentation may be just as successful and includes some valuable techniques.

Direct upstream or downstream presentations run the risk of lining the trout, either when the upstream presentation lands or when the downstream presentation passes overhead. Slightly offsetting the cast is the easiest remedy for this. Quartering the fly downstream and following its drift with the rod tip will allow you to maintain contact with the fly. You still want to introduce S curves into the leader to help fight drag. And you want to cast so that the fly lands outside of the trout's cone of sight. This can be done by estimating the depth of water where the fish is and moving approximately 14 inches away from directly over its head for every foot of water depth. So if the fish is in 5 feet of water, you cast the fly to land at least 70 inches (5 times 14), or about 6 feet, upstream of the fish. This will allow the fly to land, however awkwardly, without a critical review by the trout. Immediately before the fly lands, haul the line, overpower the cast, or introduce a wiggle to add S curves. Any of these methods will work; it is a matter of preference. Once the fly has landed, keep the rod in a relatively high position, around 11 o'clock, then gradually lower the rod as the drift proceeds. This allows the addition of slack to keep from dragging the fly across the surface. During the drift from quartered to fully downstream, you may determine the need for corrective measures to counter drag by watching the fly and any objects floating around it, rather than watching the line.

For a good downstream dead-drift dry-fly presentation, you need to evaluate the current lanes and use the right leader and cast to produce the desired S curves. You should be more concerned with the effect of drag on the fly, rather than the line; the fly should move at approximately the same speed as materials floating around it. If they move together, then cross paths, then move together again, where currents would not normally be expected to cause this, you clearly have too much drag. You might throw more line into the drift or mend the line slightly to reduce the drag, but keep the amount of line on the surface to a minimum with the rod tip, if possible.

Once the line is on the water, the downstream method allows you to add line to lengthen the drift or counter drag. It is important to add line to the drift before drag straightens out the leader; though you can easily add S curves to the line when letting it out by wiggling the rod tip from side to side, it is nearly impossible to add S curves to the leader once it straightens out in the downstream drift.

One very useful method of adding slack S curves to the fly line in downstream dry-fly presentation—or any presentation, for that matter—is to roll-cast slack into the line. Strip off approximately twice the amount of line you want to add to the drift, and hold it in your line hand. Allow this line to feed out as you bring the rod up to roll-cast, and continue to feed the line from there to the cast, rather than pulling the line from the water, which would straighten it out and defeat the whole purpose. Then under-power the roll cast so that the loop collapses upon completion. This method adds slack to the drift, and if you use it when drifting the fly in a path that is not exactly downstream from you, it effectively forces the added slack to jump over any current lanes between you and the lane in which the fly is drifting.

Another important consideration in any downstream method is the strike. When you are directly or nearly directly upstream of a trout, it is likely that a quick strike will pull the fly out of the fish's mouth before the hook is set. For this reason, you should set the hook by making a sideways flip of the rod tip in combination with a slight strip of the line. If you are able to tell the direction the fish moves, the rod tip should go in the opposite direction. The fish will usually move toward deeper water or cover, but do not be surprised if it comes directly at you, and be prepared to strip in line.

What you do once you have detected drag is also important. Your immediate reaction may be to abort the effort, pick up the line, and try again. This is probably the worst thing to do. Picking up the line and fly creates a disturbance and is likely to put the fish down. One alternative is to continue the drift, allowing the fly to swing in the current like a wet fly. It may surprise you to see how often you catch fish this way. But these are trout, not physicists.

A third, more active, alternative is to use what we know about insects to mimic their behavior. This is the fly fisherman's version of puppet theater. Just be sure to keep things in the proper scale. If you have drag, you can rarely mend line and leader enough to restore a dead drift without creating too much surface disturbance. But what you can do is impart movement to the fly. Leonard Wright, in *Trout Maverick,* describes a technique he calls the "sudden inch." Here you apply a small movement to the dry fly on a scale appropriate for the insect's size and potential activity. The idea is to keep the fly moving as if it were a natural trying to fight the pull of the current. Then the drag itself becomes part of the drama the trout sees, enticing him to end the misery of the poor, struggling insect caught in treacherous currents. You can use a variety of movements, from the sudden inch to gradual slow finger-twist retrieves, particularly good on slow-moving water. A sudden pull of the line with the rod tip down will pull the fly underwater, and you then have the opportunity to simulate either a drowning fly or, if the fly has been dressed or is buoyant, a fly that emerges from the surface film to ride atop the water. All of these movements mask the fact that the fly is being acted on by drag.

The Riffling Hitch, Surface Skipping, and Dapping
The riffling hitch, a useful method for controlling the drift of surface or near-surface flies, imparts movement to dry flies fished on a tight line.

The technique involves tying one or two half-hitch knots after the initial knot between the tippet and fly. Slip the half-hitch backward behind the eye of the hook and onto the head wrappings of the fly. This allows the leader more direct control of the fly—the farther back from the eye, the greater the control. The line, leader, and fly are typically dressed with floatant, allowing the fly to be lifted or even bounced off the surface. You can drift the fly with the current, strip it in a retrieve, or allow it to swing on the end of the leader with or without surface disturbance or wake.

Fisherman use this technique for fish in riffles or water with moderate current, imparting movement to a dry fly either to entice a territorial fish to strike or to simulate the natural behavior of a fly trapped in the surface film or drifting downstream. It exaggerates the behavior of a fly surrendering to drag, through the use of a tight line and induced movement. Occasionally twitch the fly or even strip it in to produce a wake on the water's surface. For trout, the size of the wake should be minimal, as no natural fly is capable of creating a water skier's rooster tail. The stillwater of a lake is less suitable for this technique, because flies can often walk on the water's surface if not disturbed by current.

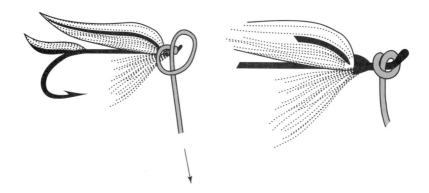

Riffling Hitch

It may surprise you to see a fish that has ignored or refused more than one dead-drift presentation turn and attack a fly presented at the surface with some movement. But the amount of movement should be appropriate for the natural and should not be constant; for example, you might follow a single twitch by several seconds of patient drift. The amount of movement should depend on the fly. Bushy stoneflies, grasshoppers, and caddisflies are notoriously active, and movement should mimic this behavior. Mayflies, on the other hand, tend to move very little in the course of the drift, often simply pirouetting from time to time; at emergence, however, they often struggled to shed their skins. It is this behavior that attracts trout to a moving fly during some mayfly hatches.

Surface skipping is the same technique taken to the extreme. Fishermen usually use a caddis imitation for this method. Treat the fly as for a riffle hitch, but pull it up and allow it to leave and return to the water from time to time. This technique may also be used on stillwater where caddis activity is present. Strikes sometimes occur after a fly has left the water's surface, so pay close attention. You might alternate periods of activity with dead drift to simulate the active and still patterns of a caddis.

This practice is particularly enjoyable when a light wind is at your back. Even when you have drag, you may be able to reset the S curves. Using a line, leader, and fly dressed with floatant, make your initial cast. When it becomes evident that your fly is dragging, try timing a quick lift of the rod tip with a light breeze going from you toward the fly. As the wind picks up the line, it will flip the leader and fly, allowing the leader to relax from the drag of the water; as it drops gently back down to the water, the S curves are restored. If you use a lighter line, say a 3- or even a 2-weight, you can aerialize the line and most of the leader with little effort and bounce the fly on the surface, behavior that can cause trout to perform spectacular acrobatics in their pursuit. I have seen trout come completely out of the water after flies presented in this fashion and strike in midair, and it takes great control not to pull back too soon. In most instances, you expect trout to take the fly from below, but it is as common for them to take the fly on their way down with this presentation. Again, it seems to work best on very calm water, which may be because of improved visibility and lower surface tension on the line by the water. You do not have a great deal of control under these circumstances, but when it works, it is quite a scene, and it makes you look like a fly-casting virtuoso.

Irish lough (lake) fishermen use real mayflies on a #12 or #14 hook and a similar technique that has been called dapping. This method calls for using a long rod, over 11 feet, usually from a drifting boat or along the bank of a lake. The fly is bounced off the surface at the end of a nylon line, inducing the fish to take the fly as it hits the surface or even as it leaves the water. The strikes may be quite dramatic, as fish will leave the water entirely to go after the fly.

Pocket Water and High Sticking

Pocket water refers to relatively small pockets of holding water in the areas between boulders, surrounded by sometimes frothing turbulent current. Pocket water can be present on small streams or large rivers. The Madison River in Montana and the Muskegon River in Michigan are over 100 feet wide in places where boulder-strewn bottoms form pocket water situations. Smaller streams with high gradients and rough bottoms can produce pocket water with currents that swirl in every direction. Visibility is often limited by the turbulence and bubbles, so stealth is not always necessary, but a small window of stiller water may provide fish with the opportunity to detect your presence. Careful wading should be the rule, not only for safety, but to avoid sending out warnings to fish from sand and boulders grinding against each other or clouds of silt and sand floating downstream.

Because of the complex currents found in pocket water you cannot expect to achieve long, drag-free drifts. The solution is to target pockets behind and in front of boulders, where fish may find refuge from the stronger current. Fish will seek such places and use them to rest while waiting for the current to bring food to them, just beyond the relative safety of the pocket.

High sticking is so named because the presentation is made with the rod tip held high. The fly is targeted to close pockets. Little or no line is in contact with the water, because the rod tip holds the line off the water during the short drift. This allows the fly to drift with less drag, especially if followed by the rod tip, because the leader is less prone than line to be affected by the current because of its smaller diameter and consequently lower surface area in contact with the water.

Although most commonly used with nymphs, this technique can be successful with virtually any type of fly. If you are fishing the fly on a relatively tight line, a strike indicator is not necessary. If, however, you are making a dead-drift presentation, this is usually done with some sort of strike indicator. Fish cannot be very selective under these conditions, because food items move past them at high speeds, so takes may occur at any time. Fish use their mouths as tactile organs, so they may take first to check the fly out, then spit it out quickly if not satisfied that it is food. So quick action and reaction on your part are the rules of the game.

The typical cast is made quartering upstream. Aim the rod tip at the end of the fly line and follow the drift with it. Hold the rod tip nearly level when the line is upstream. As the line drifts to a position directly across current, raise the tip so that the fly travels in the same current lane in which it began its drift. Then, as it passes, lower the rod tip to keep it in the same lane. Once you have cast the fly, you may want to have the rod precede the fly and leader downstream so that any drag goes with the current rather than against it, which likely will make the fly appear more natural than if it were making some sort of bizarre effort to fight a raging current.

Stripping Streamers and Woolly Buggers

Stripping subsurface patterns such as streamers or Woolly Buggers can be an effective way of inducing strong strikes from large trout. These fish require bigger meals to maintain their size, so consequently, they are more likely to go after a larger imitation than a small surface fly. Using the leader formulas presented earlier, sized for the line and the fly, you can cast a Woolly Bugger or streamer quartering upstream and allow it to drift. Take up most of the slack as the fly drifts. You may occasionally strip or add movements to the fly as it proceeds downstream.

In stripping patterns meant to represent minnows, crayfish, leeches, or other creatures capable of a fair degree of mobility, you need to consider the degree to which these creatures can fight a current. A 1-inch crayfish is not likely to be able to swim upstream against the midchannel current of a large river, yet stripping a Wooly Bugger in this water can produce fish. A 15-inch trout is not likely to take on an 8-inch fish that could swim upstream against such a current, but the trout may recognize the Woolly Bugger as a high-calorie meal that is not a significant threat. It is best to make your presentation as natural as possible, so strip streamers or Woolly Buggers downstream for the most part. And a minnow or crayfish is not prone to attack a trout, so you should not strip flies, large or small, toward trout. This is an aggressive and abnormal behavior that will not only confuse, but frighten, even very large fish.

A drift on a nearly tight line, followed with the rod tip, and occasionally stripped in, will often produce strikes. Once the streamer or Woolly Bugger has reached the downstream position, you may want to try either leaving it hang in the current or dropping it farther downstream by slowly adding slack. Then retrieve.

Retrievals vary. Some advocate 6-inch strips; others use a finger twist, inching the line in with the fingers. Wildly stripping line in 2 feet at a time has even worked in nonturbulent water where erratic behavior by wounded or startled minnows or crayfish may cause large predators to move in for the kill. Keep track of the line you strip in so it does not become a tangled mess that you cannot manage during a fight with a large fish. When stripping in line lengths more than a few inches at a time, keep the line between your index finger and the rod. Then, if there is a quick strike, you can close your finger on the line to set the hook as you move the rod tip.

To more accurately portray the natural movement of baitfish or crayfish, you may want to use a weight sufficient to keep the fly down yet still allow it to bounce downstream at a rate just slower than the current. The weight will allow the fly to hesitate in its drift from time to time, just as a natural might in moving about on the bottom of the stream.

SUBSURFACE METHODS
Weighted Flies and Split Shot
Fly fishermen disagree over whether it is more appropriate to weight a nymph or add weight to the leader to sink the fly to the desired depth. The addition of beadheads to the fly-tying arena in recent years has brought in another element to the discussion. But a beadhead is just an intermediate to the other two alternatives, like attaching a split shot to the head of the nymph. The advantage of shiny beadheads is that they tend to be attractors or to mimic the wing case or gases trapped in the wing case of a nymph. But they are primarily a weight, nonetheless.

A nymph can be weighted by using lead or tungsten wire under the dressing. An older method is to use lead foil, often obtained from the seals of wine corks or the stoppers in other liquid inspirations shared by fly tiers in days of old. Lead or tin foil have almost universally been replaced by plastic or aluminum, but they are still available and have the advantage of allowing some degree of creativity in shape not as easily achieved with wire. If you want to tie low-profile weighted nymphs, you can use a hard rolling pin and a countertop to flatten lead or tungsten wire, but once you have used a rolling pin for lead, do not use it again for food.

The argument against weighted nymphs is based on a comparison between the relative weights of naturals and artificials, and the effect that additional weight has on drift. One difference between naturals and artificials is that naturals are usually coming off the bottom, whereas artificials descend through the water column, at least initially. So the problem is how to make artificials move like the naturals. A weighted nymph will, if sufficiently weighted, hit the bottom and bounce, much like a natural. But there are cases where a small nymph cannot be weighted enough for this to happen, or where the current is so strong that even a large, heavily weighted nymph will not stay down. In such cases, external weight is appropriate.

When using external weight, you need to place it so that the path taken by the fly simulates a natural. If the nymph is small, the current will dictate the way a natural moves. So the imitation should not behave as though such a small creature is able to battle a current and move about with the same degree of control as the trout. Place enough weight six inches or so from the nymph to get the nymph down. Use no more weight than absolutely necessary, as the nymph should appear to be tumbling pretty much out of control.

If you encounter a situation where nymphs are present near the surface, and you want to have the option of fishing your nymph anywhere in the water column, you may want to consider an unweighted nymph and add small to large split shot or other weight to adjust the depth. As an alternative to this, some tiers tie variably weighted nymphs and color code the thread for weightless, moderate, or heavy weight. This requires carrying more flies and changing flies, both of which can interfere with your fishing. An effective alternative is to fish both a near-surface and a deeper form of the same fly together in tandem.

If you fish with heavily weighted flies or add split shot to your leaders, some cautions are in order. Not only are weights inelegant and a nuisance to cast, but they can be dangerous to you or your rod. Graphite is very susceptible to shattering if hit by hard, fast-moving objects like split shot or a weighted #4 Matuka. If you hit your rod with a weight, it may crack enough to shatter the next time you catch a fish. The longer the rod, the faster your line is likely to be moving, and it is conceivable that your line and leader, and anything you have on it, are moving at speeds close to 70 miles per hour. Not only is that sufficient to shatter a rod, but it can embed a hook into nearly any part of your body. Be careful. The experience of removing a large, weighted nymph that is buried in your flesh will add to the already strong motivation to use barbless hooks.

SETTING THE HOOK

With all of the slack and **S** curves in the leader, how do you set the hook? This is a reasonable question. Although one often fishes to relax, you need to be attentive, and quick reaction is an essential element in success. Keep your line hand on the line; that is the starting point. If there is a strike, most fishermen respond with the rod first, only retrieving line after the hook is set. The presumption is that the rod will prevent the leader from breaking by acting as a shock absorber, which it will. But the result of this sequence—fish strikes, fisherman raises rod to set hook, then retrieves line—is that the rod too often is in a vertical position before the hook is really set and retrieval starts. Then, if the fish charges toward you, you wind up frantically stripping in line, and awkwardly trying to get the rod as high in the air as possible to keep tension on the fish. Many fish are caught this way in spite of the very awkward "dance" that results. The spectacle of a frantic fisherman with his rod as high over his head as he can reach, clumsily stepping backward to maintain tension on the fish in the "midstream cutthroat waltz," is not how we like to envision ourselves when we fly-fish.

A preferred method is to keep your eyes on the fly and the leader, and your line hand on the line. When you suspect a strike or a subtle take, immediately use your line hand to retrieve the line and take out the slack with a quick tug or line strip. Do so while holding the line just tightly enough to strip it, but loosely enough that as soon as the fish tugs back, the line slips with some resistance between your fingers. Once you sense that the fish is hooked, you can start playing it, maintaining tension either with your fingers or by quickly reeling in the slack and using the drag of the reel. This method has the immediate advantage of leaving the fly in the water—in case you were mistaken and there was no strike, or if the fish is quicker than you, and spits out the fly—so you can continue to let the fly drift, should you wish to do so. I have caught fish that have spit out a fly, only to return and strike with vigor upon seeing it move when I made a quick, short tug of the line hand. The second reason for setting the hook in this fashion is that it takes the slack out of the line before the rod is raised, allowing you the full utility of the rod in fighting the fish. If you do not have the slack out of the line when you first set the hook, you have the rod up and in the air before the fish is on. In this situation, you cannot use the rod to its fullest, because you cannot pull it back any farther. If you take up the slack first, then pull up the tip, you have the full flex of the rod at your disposal to play the fish.

You may find yourself breaking tippets if you have gone all day without a fish and are then surprised by a sudden strike. If you continually fail to hook fish with this technique, it is possible your hooks are dull and you need to sharpen them. An easy way to check hook sharpness is to drag the fly, hook down, across your thumbnail. If it is dull, the hook will skate across, barely leaving a scratch. If it is sharp, the point should easily hang up and start to embed itself into your fingernail when gently dragged across it, though this is not to say you need to perforate your fingernail with every fly you tie on. An obvious set of skills is required to execute this technique, but once you develop the ability to set the hook as described, you will easily get from the strike to a comfortable, enjoyable position with your rod in relation to the fish.

CHAPTER 11

The Leader as a Line

Astandard fly line, if used on small, fast-flowing streams with lots of pocket water or highly variable currents, will quickly develop drag. By using monofilament as the line and leader, the cross-sectional area that is acted on by the complex currents is significantly reduced, and so, consequently, are the effects of drag. Following the nymph's course in the drift with the rod tip held high and waiting for the slightest indication of a take can be a very effective way of cleaning out fish in fast, boulder-strewn sections of water.

Casting without a fly line is not particularly picturesque or elegant, and some places, such as European angling clubs, may have restrictions against techniques such as those described in this chapter. But an understanding of the importance of reducing drag and the increase in fishing on spring creeks have led to consideration of the lineless casting method for situations where conventional techniques have limited success.

Using monofilament has several advantages on spring creeks. Because they are small by nature, long casts are wasted effort. The high visibility of a rod waving back and forth with an opaque line following it is difficult to conceal from the view of fish in shallow, clear water. In direct contrast, using a single casting motion, with no false casting, and a clear monofilament line reduces the chances of spooking fish. The monofilament is also less prone to heavy impact on the water surface, adding to its utility where stealth is critical. A monofilament line will not cast as noticeable a shadow as a conventional fly line, so overhead lining of fish is not as great a concern. And the lightness of a monofilament line helps minimize drag during the drift.

Using the no-line methods effectively requires a light rod, something less than a 5-weight. Length may be dictated by availability and the possibility of snagging brush with the rod. Bear in mind that every foot of rod is one more foot between you and the fish, and the effect of a longer rod as a lever allows you to develop higher line speed. A mathematical formula can be used to show what you may already know from practical experience or common sense. If you consider the rotation of the arm and rod in the forward cast from 2 o'clock to 10 o'clock, you can estimate the effect of rod length on the loop speed. The hand goes from 2 o'clock to 10 o'clock in, say, one second. The arc of a 2-foot radius over that distance, assuming the distance from your elbow to the handle of the rod is 2 feet, is

$$(2\ \pi\ r) \times \tfrac{1}{3} \text{ or } (4\ \pi) \times \tfrac{1}{3} = 4.2 \text{ ft.}$$

because the distance from 2 o'clock to 10 o'clock is one-third of the circle of the clock.

The arc length is approximately 4.2 feet and, combined with a travel time of one second, yields 4.2 feet per second. Using the same formula and considerations with a 7-foot rod, resulting in an arc with a radius of approximately 9 feet, the line at the tip in the forward cast is moving at 19 feet per second. For an 8-foot rod, this becomes 21 feet per second, and for a 9-foot rod, it becomes 23 feet per second. So adding 1 foot to the length adds about 2 feet per second, or 1.3 miles per hour, to the line speed at the tip. The same relationship between length of radius and arc length is the reason military march steps are standardized lengths; otherwise soldiers of different heights with differing leg lengths would be marching at different speeds.

Some writers advocate taking the fly line off the reel before using monofilament as a fly line, believing that a large fish may pull the monofilament into the line, either burying it in the coils of line and causing the leader to break, or damaging the line if a sudden run occurs. But you can control most fish in the short term with your fingers as a drag on the line; after all, these are trout, not 5-foot tarpon. Besides, it is nearly impossible to keep the monofilament from acquiring memory coils if you wind it up onto the spool rather than keep it loose. If you do hook a huge fish, there may be the potential of being cut or burned by the monofilament if you do not have a chance to use the drag, and theoretically you could cut a finger. But think of the stories you could tell to explain such a mishap! I recommend loop-connecting the monofilament onto the fly line, which then becomes the backing.

TAPER DESIGN

Using monofilament as both line and leader is not likely to be something you set out to do at the start of an outing, but a kind of emergency adaptation to conditions at hand. If, on thinking ahead, you realize that you will be using this method, you may want to design a special line just for this use. Such a line would incorporate the principles of the convex tapered leader, with lengthened sections. You could prepare the following line for a 3- to 4-weight rod, and keep it in your field leader kit or vest in a plastic bag for just such emergencies:

Monofilament Line for 3- to 4-Weight Rod

Diameter (inches)	Length (inches)
0.019	48
0.021	60
0.023	72
0.019	36
0.015	12
0.013	12
0.011	12
0.009	12
0.007	12
0.006	24-28

If, while on a stream, you see the need to quickly fabricate a line for this method, you can simplify the design without losing much efficiency. Because it functions as both the line and the energy transfer taper, the starting diameter of monofilament should be sized just as if it were a transition between the energy transfer taper and the line. A section of line from 0.016 to 0.025 inch will do, depending on the stiffness of the rod, as much as anything else. The initial section should be roughly the width of the creek or the length of the longest cast you may realistically expect to make, and no more. Additional line will increase the potential for tangles, and you are unlikely to ever cast more than 30 feet effectively with this setup. Work the entire line over by pulling it under tension to straighten it as much as possible. You may also want to consider dressing it with a paste floatant.

The transition taper should be sufficient to step down between the starting diameter of the monofilament and the presentation taper. You may wish to use the depth of the deepest pool in a spring creek as a ballpark value for length. For the transition taper, 4 to 6 feet may be as good a starting point as any. The taper is important, as it will perform functions of energy transfer necessary for turnover and will help control drag. Using the diameter of the presentation section based on the fly size, a transition section of four to six equal-length segments stepping down in equal increments to the presentation section will perform these functions well. For example, consider stepping down from a line of 0.019-inch monofilament to a 5X (0.006-inch) presentation section. Using a 6-foot transition taper and six equal segments, this gives you a configuration of 12-inch segments in 0.017, 0.015, 0.013, 0.011, 0.009, and 0.007. That makes for a lot of knot tying, but it will result in a leader that will produce S curves and turn over fairly well with some casting practice. Do your practicing on water you do not intend to fish.

The diameter of the presentation section should be sized according to the fly. Its length should be based on the flow rate of the water. Dead still-water has no drag to it, so the presentation section may be as short as 24 inches. Water that is nearly still, but has complex currents, warrants a presentation section from 24 to 30 inches. Faster water may require a presentation section from 30 to 40 inches. If you are fishing nymphs in water with visible current, the presentation section should be approximately one and a half times the water depth. This will allow the nymph to reach the bottom of the water column, and you will be close enough to watch the rest of the leader and the fish itself to detect strikes.

CASTING

With some adjustments, you will find that casting dynamics are similar with a monofilament line on a light rod as with a fly line, although at a smaller scale, with the major exceptions being that loading the rod, shooting line, and hauling are simply not possible. The need to use this method implies the need for stealth, so the pickup from the water surface should be smooth and calm to minimize spray and surface disturbance. You also should limit yourself to a single backcast—no false casting unless absolutely necessary to get line out. Apply extra power to the last part of the backcast, continuing through the forward cast, as the angular momentum induced by the movement of a conventional line is not there to power the forward cast. Although considered by some a cardinal sin in conventional casting, additional acceleration needed to turn the line over may be achieved by snap-flexing the wrist in the forward cast after the line has straightened out behind you. This deviation in form is a small compensation for the loss of the ability to haul the line.

Casting heavily weighted nymphs or using split shot with this method can be problematic, because the line is not stiff enough to turn over much weight. Unless you are casting less than 10 feet, which amounts to flipping the weighted nymph, you should seriously minimize the amount of weight used. If you choose to use split shot, select the absolute smallest size. The weight of a nymph and/or split shot may be sufficient to actually shoot some line, but consider the tendency for monofilament to coil and tangle before risking a catastrophic failure.

The selection of leader material for its relative flexibility is more critical when the leader is also functioning as a line. The energy transfer section and transition taper should be of relatively stiff material to achieve turnover, especially when you are using weighted flies. The presentation section should be very flexible, as you will be using this method in areas where stealth is essential.

THE BOW-AND-ARROW CAST

Several authors have written of the merits of casting a monofilament line and leader where stealth, drag reduction, and close quarters are considerations. One method described for use in close quarters is the bow-and-arrow cast, which calls for stripping off enough line for the cast and loading the rod manually by pulling the fly back and letting it go. It has limited range and is difficult to execute well without practice. Take care and use barbless hooks, as you can easily hook yourself while performing the bow-and-arrow cast. Still, it allows the fly to be cast beneath tight, overhanging brush or in other close quarters.

Most references to the bow-and-arrow cast advise turning the rod handle so that the rod is flexed in the same direction as it is when landing a fish. This notion is possibly based on the spline of the rod, which is typically oriented so that the rod flexes most easily in this direction. Flexing a rod in any other direction will stress it in a manner that can result in rotational torque, and in extreme cases when using cane rods, the rod can sustain structural damage. Under the limited flexure for the bow-and-arrow casts, however, there is little risk of this occurring.

To perform the cast, pull out the leader a distance approximating the length of the rod. Carefully pull back the fly to load the rod, while holding the reel spool to prevent additional line from unspooling. Align the rod tip with the target, and aim it at an angle approximately 45 degrees for a first try. Release the fly, which shoots toward the target in an arc. If you pulled the line back too far, resulting in too much tension on the rod, the fly will hit the surface only inches in front of the rod tip with a resounding splat, scaring any fish in the vicinity. If you did not tension the rod enough, the fly will fall downward before the line extends, essentially underpowered by the cast. The cast has the ability to be arced either right or left simply by orienting the rod appropriately. This is very useful in getting the fly under low overhangs. The keys to the successful bow-and-arrow cast are practice and knowing its limitations.

Close quarters and a lot of brush may call for bow-and-arrow casting.
There are fish in such streams, but these situations require short casts.

It is normally sufficient to use the leader already on the line, rather than tailoring a specific leader for this cast. Bear in mind the need to maintain a fairly limp or soft tippet, owing to the stealthy, low-drag requirements of this type of fishing, balanced by the realization that you are likely to snag overhanging branches from time to time.

CHAPTER 12

Nymph Presentation

Trout obtain more than half of their calories from subsurface food, and with the exception of fish large enough to feed on smaller fish, this primarily means nymphs. There is a greater food supply below the surface than on or above it. And the closer to the surface a trout moves, the more susceptible it is to predators above the surface, and even to subsurface predators, as the trout becomes more visible the closer it gets to the surface, and the number of directions it can move to avoid capture diminishes. There is a certain sense of satisfaction in enticing a fish to come into our world, at or above water, to take a fly, but it is safer for the fish to lie low. So, although some find fishing dry flies and being able to see the takes more enjoyable, the simple fact is that dry-fly fishermen are fighting against the odds most of the time.

For the purposes of this discussion, nymph patterns include those designed specifically to imitate various developmental stages of mobile but immature aquatic life forms incapable of flight, such as larvae and pupae. This also may include emergers, but it excludes streamers, wet flies, scuds, egg patterns, and marabou jigs, as the characteristics of nymphs differ significantly from those of non-nymph subsurface patterns.

With regard to the methods and leaders used to fish them, nymphs fall into several groups: unweighted small nymphs, weighted small nymphs, large nymphs, and emergers. Emergers and unweighted small nymphs essentially behave the same, unless you use external weight in the form of split shot or strip weight. Large nymphs may be weighted or not, but because of their size and general weight, they are grouped together.

You can use a greater variety of connections in nymph presentation than in delicate dry-fly leaders, because visibility and surface impact are not as much of a factor. The use of loop connections is common, as they allow quick easy adjustment of segment lengths to compensate for differing depths of water. The angle between the joined segments at a knot can also be used to advantage in nymph leaders. You can use the tag end of one segment to attach indicators, and changing from the straight-line geometry of a blood knot to a right-angle approach is just a matter of altering which segment of line is longer. Using a right-angle setup keeps the indicator more directly above the fly than in a conventional arrangement.

The variations of technique and the application of leader characteristics to nymph fishing warrant detailed consideration. There are a few different methods of fishing nymphs: dead-drift nymphing, which is based on avoiding drag; emerger techniques; tight-line nymphing, which uses drag as part of the presentation; and heavy-weighted nymphing, which has its own unique set of techniques.

DEAD-DRIFT NYMPHING

Although nymphs are capable of locomotion, they are highly susceptible to currents. Dead-drift nymphing techniques were devised to minimize the effects of subsurface drag and make the fly appear as natural as possible.

Although trout will move some distance to intercept drifting nymphs when food is in short supply, the fish must compensate for any excess expenditure of energy by the size or calorie content of the food. So when food is relatively abundant, trout will establish a waiting position from which they can move with minimal energy expenditure to catch food that drifts by. These are known as feeding lanes, or lies. Identification of feeding lanes is a key element in successful nymph fishing. Getting the nymph to follow the current into a feeding lane in a way that the trout perceives as natural is the real challenge. Part of this involves getting the fly to the proper depth. You also need to be able to detect what sometimes tend to be subtle takes. These elements make up the essence of dead-drift nymphing.

The use of dead-drift nymphing rigs has developed into quite a specialty in recent years. Anglers have used various combinations of weights, bobbers, strike indicators, complex leaders, and weighted or unweighted flies for all kinds of conditions. Traditionalists may brand all practitioners of these inelegant techniques as heretics. But rather than stating that a method is right or wrong, this discussion will describe the purposes of various techniques, and where and how they work best, and leave you to apply this knowledge according to your own preferences.

RIGHT-ANGLE NYMPHING

Right-angle nymphing is a dead-drift method that uses floating line and a leader designed to force a hinged connection between the energy transfer section and the remainder of the leader. This allows the fly to hang in the current below a float that functions as both a buoy and an indicator. The right-angle geometry assures a more accurate indication of the location of the fly by the float as well. The formulas for these leaders are such that the drag on the vertical portion is lower than in conventional leaders to reduce downstream bowing of the underwater portions.

You cast the nymph upstream and across with the right-angle leader, then throw an immediate mend into the line to assist in getting the fly to drop to the feeding depth before it is dragged by the float and line. The amount of weight needed to get the fly to the feeding zone varies with current and the weighting of the nymph; however, because of the efficiency of the leader geometry, less weight is necessary than might be used with conventional leaders. This means easier casting, easier mending, easier differentiation between strikes and hang-ups, and more natural drift of the fly.

The use of loop connections is convenient and allows the connection of segments of varying lengths, but unless you plan on carrying and stowing a variety of lengths of looped segments in your leader wallet, this is a marginal consideration. The strength of loop connections is an advantage, but well-tied and tested knots can be nearly as good. Still, if you are using fluorocarbon for the underwater portions of the leader and colored nylon for the floating butt section, you are better off with looped connections because of the combination of contrasting materials and diameters. A double overhand knot tied with the tag ends even and together, rather than overlapping, will result in an acute angle that also works well between the energy transfer and underwater segments. A 3- to 4-inch tag end of a knot or loop between the butt and the underwater sections makes a good point of attachment for a float.

Rigging

Nymphing is usually done with floating lines. This is because of the inconvenience of changing spools to change methods and the simple fact that they work better for this type of fishing. Sinking lines or sinking tips cause greater disturbance when they are pulled from the water to begin a cast, and the added weight used may make casting even more awkward than with the complicated arrangement of weight and floats. A floating line allows more control, as it is easier to mend during the drift. Strike detection is also aided by a floating line, as you are able to feel the floating line drift more than you might one that drags on the bottom or hangs up on subsurface irregularities.

As with any leader, the energy transfer taper for dead-drift nymphing must be stiff enough to transfer the energy from the line to the leader, but the efficiency of the energy transfer becomes more critical with the extra weight and air resistance of nymphing setups. If you use weighted nymphs or split shot, the added air resistance of these items, combined with that of a strike indicator, will require special attention in leader design and casting techniques. The energy transfer section should be sized at the upper limits of the general guidelines given earlier—it should be no greater than 60 percent the diameter of the end of the fly line.

The best energy transfer between line and leader occurs with a knotted connection. A needle-knotted section of monofilament that is 60 percent the diameter of the tip of the line works well. If you do not like the near permanence of such an attachment to the line, you may consider using a segment of monofilament that will work well as the first segment of the energy transfer section for most of your leaders, and put a loop on the end of it. A 2- or 3-foot segment of properly sized Amnesia or other colored line, in either red or fluorescent green, performs well as a strike and drift indicator and can form the first segment of either wet- or dry-fly leaders.

A loop connection at the end of the first segment will be less critical to leader performance, because the need for efficient energy transfer decreases closer to the fly. The next segment in this setup is one case where it is actually desirable to have a hinge in your leader, and a loop connection will accomplish this. A loop connection also allows you a place to tie on a segment to attach a float, should you prefer not to have the adhesive of a stick-on foam indicator on the semipermanent butt section. Another option is to tie a strike indicator such as a poly-yarn wad onto the end of the energy transfer section, and attach the transition taper to the energy transfer section at a right angle with either a loop knot or an improved clinch knot, resulting in a forced hinge.

The transition taper for this setup is fairly simple. This section consists of two equal segments with a total length of one and a half to two times the depth at which you plan to drift your fly—one and a half in relatively slow water, two in faster water. The diameters are at equal intervals between the energy transfer section and the presentation section.

The presentation section of a nymphing setup is based on the size of nymph and whether or not it is weighted, internally or by split shot. A 24- to 30-inch segment of moderately stiff, properly sized tippet should suffice.

Technique

Casting a dead-drift nymph, or any nymph for that matter, is a best done with a minimum of false casting. The fly does not need to be dried off, as it is intended to be fished subsurface, and extra false casts create more opportunity for knots and tangles. Spool off line and coil it nearby to feed out during the backcast and forward cast, rather than stripping off lengths during false casts. This will make a difference in the number of wind knots that occur in your line.

Some anglers prefer to cast nymphs quartering upstream or downstream; others promote casting nearly straight upstream or downstream. If you are casting to a specific spot or fish, it is best to think about exactly where you want the fly to be before you cast—this means where you want it to wind up, not where you want it to land. Think about how long the fly will have to sink and how much it will have to drift downstream to reach the target depth. Then consider the amount of current and the resulting drag you will have to deal with. Plan your cast according to these criteria, regardless of whether you prefer upstream or downstream casting. Learn the reach cast, practice it, and learn how to effectively mend line. Be prepared to mend a little or a lot of line immediately upon the fly hitting the water, as you may not always accurately predict the degree to which wind will alter your cast or how fast the current is really flowing. Follow the nymph with the rod tip nearly level, and with just enough slack to throw loose line into the drift if needed. Keep your line hand ready either to respond to detected drag by mending line or to strike at the slightest hesitation of the line or indicator.

You can also use high-sticking techniques for dead-drift nymphing. Keep the rod tip nearly horizontal during the portion of the drift upstream of your position. As the fly approaches, raise the rod tip to keep the line, and consequently the fly, in the same current lane. Then, as the fly passes your position and begins to move downstream, lower the rod tip to provide additional slack line.

Another technique for minimizing drag during deep subsurface fishing is described by Gary LaFontaine in *Caddisflies* as the limbo method. This method fishes nymphs or larval imitations in the first few inches to a foot above the bottom of a stream. Once you have made the cast, upstream or quartering upstream, you submerge the rod, aimed at the fly, until the tip touches the bottom. Then follow the drifting fly with the rod. This technique reduces the number of boundaries among contrasting currents that your line and leader must travel across, thereby minimizing drag and resulting in a more natural drift. LaFontaine admits that this technique is rough on equipment and recommends that it not be used with a good rod.

FISHING EMERGERS

Emergers are in transition from nymph to adult. The emergers rise in the water column and drift in the near surface or at the surface before taking wing. Emerger patterns number in the hundreds or thousands. Some represent the pupal stage as it loses its casing, freeing the wings to fly.

Emergers may be fished just as wet flies or nymphs, although some are fished as dry. Appropriate leader and casting styles depend on the stage of emergence or whether the pattern is representative of a failed emergence or drowned emerger.

When fishing an emerger, allow the fly to drop well below the surface by casting upstream and mending, just as with a nymph. Some emergers are lightly weighted to assist in sinking. Then, as with a wet fly, use the Leisenring Lift technique to raise the fly through the water column toward the surface. At the surface, allow it to hang in suspension, where, with some degree of luck, it will be taken by a trout.

TIGHT-LINE NYMPHING

Tight-line nymphing does not mean that you keep the line as taut as a piano wire, but simply that you keep close enough contact on the line that you can feel the nymph hitting the bottom of the stream or being bumped by a fish. This technique also allows you to maneuver the nymph to simulate natural behavior or to entice a fish to strike. The method also includes aspects of traditional wet-fly fishing, including following the downstream swing of the nymph in its drift, as well as the use of the Leisenring Lift to raise the nymph through the water column at the end of the drift.

Rigging

The leader should be sized to the line at the energy transfer section and to the fly at the presentation section. You will need a stiffer transition taper in order to turn over the nymph, which is normally weighted, and you may also need a stiffer presentation taper. Twisting of a finer, softer material while the nymph hangs in the current will result in irreversible curling of the tippet in a very short time.

Use a tippet one size heavier than normal when using split shot, or even thicker where you expect to encounter potential snags. The thicker tippet is not as likely to spook fish as you might think. The appropriate total leader length depends on the depth of water and the current. A good starting point is one and a half times the depth for moderate current or twice the depth for faster streams.

Technique

In tight-line nymphing, you typically cast the nymph either directly across current or slightly downstream. An immediate upstream mend will help get the fly down to the target depth. Once you believe the fly has reached the proper depth, take in enough slack to the point where you can feel the nymph in tension or bumping the bottom of the stream. Follow the drift with the rod tip in a horizontal position. If you are using a strike indicator, keep a close eye on it, and respond to any hesitation with a short strip from the line hand. Leave the rod horizontal unless you feel a real strike. This will allow you to continue the drift if the hesitation was a false alarm.

You can use minor mending to maintain depth through the drift as it approaches a position directly downstream. As the drift nears the downstream position, you may apply the Leisenring Lift to induce a strike. A couple versions of the lift have been developed over the years. The most common, and probably least imitative of the natural, simply calls for waiting until the fly is directly downstream, then gradually raising the rod tip to elevate the nymph from the deep-water position to simulate an emerging fly. The nymph will reach a straight-line position on a tight line directly downstream of you. As the nymph rises in the water column, it does so because of drag.

If you want your fly to appear more natural, you should try to simulate the ascension that occurs in the transition from nymph to emerger. If you think about how this might happen, you can use the current and the drag of the line to simulate it. A nymph cannot swim against the current in most streams; it will rise to emerge and drift downstream as it does so. Cast a mend into the line to start your nymph near the bottom. Then, before the nymph is directly downstream, slowly pull it upward while following the current in a downstream motion. You can try to get the nymph facing upstream by having the rod tip slightly upstream of the ascending fly, or facing downstream by leading the fly with your rod tip. The fly should not hold steady in the current or swim against it if you want it to appear natural.

HEAVY-WEIGHTED NYMPHING

Heavy-weighted nymphs in #10 down to #4 are awkward to cast, but they are well-suited representations of large creatures like stonefly and damselfly nymphs. The most common techniques for fishing these flies often involve variations of what has been called the "chuck-and-duck" method. This refers to the fact that you are essentially making a single backcast with an unwieldy assemblage of weighted nymph, split shot, and strike indicator and flinging it forward, trying to avoid embedding the hook in your scalp or elsewhere. The method is typically used on fast-moving freestone streams, where stonefly nymphs crawl around on the bottom of the riverbed, occasionally dislodging and tumbling downstream, or simply swimming along below the fastest currents in the protected pockets behind boulders.

Rigging

A typical "chuck-and-duck" rig is fairly simple. It usually consists of level segments that do not have any significant taper, because the fly and the split shot are so heavy that they, and not the line, provide the momentum for the cast. The first segment is a 2-foot length sized to the end of the fly line. Loop connections will speed up the process of changing segment lengths, as the segments are subject to kinking and abrasion, requiring frequent replacement. Connect a float at the union of the first segment with the rest of the leader. The middle segment is just a level portion of leader, which should be fairly stiff, but flexible enough to allow the nymph and split shot to drop through the water column and stay down. Stream depth determines the appropriate length of this segment. Use a segment one and a half times the stream depth for fairly fast water, or twice the depth for very fast water. Place a weight near the union of the middle segment and the tippet. The tippet should be about 2 feet long—allowing the nymph to move somewhat, while still anchored to the weight—and stiff enough to minimize twisting of the nymph to avoid curling. If you believe subsurface structure may snag your weight, you can attach it using a strand of rubber band so that it will either spring loose or break off without sacrificing your fly. If you need to use heavier weights, use a length of surgical tubing stuffed with split shot, tied off to the side of the tippet, so that if snagged, you will not lose your fly.

Technique

The method for heavy-weighted nymphing is simple. Stand facing approximately straight across stream, then strip off enough line to cast into a lane of current that you feel has promise, or where you have observed a feeding trout. Cast approximately 45 degrees upstream, and immediately throw an upstream mend into the line to allow the nymph to sink to the bottom. Follow the drift with your rod tip held slightly above horizontal. When the drift approaches the downstream position, lower the tip of the rod to allow a little extra drift. Keep your finger on the line so you are able to feel any hesitation, and keep a sharp eye on the float. At any hesitation, tug the rod tip in a horizontal plane downstream, if the rod is not already oriented in that direction. If you pull upstream, you run a high risk of pulling the nymph out of the trout's mouth. If you pull the rod tip up, you have a higher chance of success than with an upstream tug, but if there is not a fish, you may destroy the rest of the drift by raising the fly into the fastest and most drag-prone current. By tugging downstream or allowing the current to do so, you also simulate the path a nymph would take—the path of least resistance, whether swimming under its own power or drifting out of control.

CHAPTER 13

Fly Fishing from a Boat

F ly fishing from a boat has some advantages over fly fishing from a bank or while wading. The most obvious advantage is the ability to cover larger areas of water with less effort in terms of the length of casting or the amount of foot travel. Other advantages include the ability to reach areas not otherwise possible, even with the greatest of casting; the ability to cover water without disturbing the river or lake bottom; and the tremendous increase in backcasting room.

DRIFT FISHING
Fishing from a drifting boat, flowing down a stream, has become more popular with the development of tailwater trout fisheries in the West, but the techniques have been around for some time. Drift fishing in a stream, whether from a canoe, conventional boat, or McKenzie drift boat, typically involves casting from a seated or standing position while a boatman uses oars to steer or control the boat's drift downstream. It is almost impossible to fish effectively from a drift boat if you are also trying to steer the boat. This is usually the task of a hired guide. In the case where two or three fishermen share the drift, you can take turns manning the oars.

Other than access and stealth, the major advantage to drift fishing is the control of line drift. The line is cast from a boat moving downstream, so it is already moving at a velocity mimicking that of the stream. This has several positive implications. In a conventional cast to a stream from a stationary position, the line at the end of the cast stops its forward motion (except when shooting line) and settles to the water moving beneath it. Because the water is moving downstream and the line is not, and because the water has some surface tension, the line's impact on the water will cause some disturbance. When cast from a boat moving downstream, the line, even if stopped at the end of the cast relative to the caster, is still moving downstream at the rate of travel of the boat, which is essentially the same as the stream. The line already has a downstream velocity much closer to that of the moving stream, when it settles on the water, resulting in less disturbance of the surface.

Another advantage is that because you, the rod, and the cast are all moving with the current, there is minimal drag. There is not the instantaneous contrast between the current in the stream and the resistance of the line and leader to that current that causes drag. If you cast from a stationary position, you must make adjustments in the line and use slack to compensate for drag. If you and the rod are drifting with the current, there is no stationary pivot point to cause drag. You and your line can drift along with the current without causing drag at all. The S curves in your line can be maintained almost indefinitely on a long stretch of stream, resulting in dead drifts of hundreds of feet. Drift fishing allows even a mediocre caster to produce dead drifts, because the drift does not rely on S curves to compensate for drag. It also makes up for leader designs that result in excessively straight casts or casting techniques that straighten out line to gain distance.

Things seem to happen fast when you are drifting down a trout stream, so you should be aware of where your line is every second. Running over your fly line can ruin it as it tangles and gets pulled into tight knots, and your rod can be damaged or lost if your line hangs up on a log or boulder. A floating line is preferable to a sinking line, both for visibility and casting. You will often be sight-casting to a location and must be able to react quickly, and a sinking-tip line limits your ability to quickly pick up and recast to a fish or a lie that you are passing at a fast clip. A sinking line is also more prone to hang-ups on submerged obstacles, and snags become more of a hazard when you are moving. A fly rod will not withstand the downstream momentum of a drift boat, and if you are not quick to free-spool your line in such cases, disaster may result.

LAKE FISHING

The large, windswept lakes (loughs in Ireland and lochs in Scotland) of northern Europe are often fished from boats using wet-fly techniques. Boats for this type of fishing normally have an outboard motor to get the boat to the upwind side of the productive water to be drifted. Once at the upwind side, the motor is killed and the boat positioned perpendicular to the prevailing wind. The wind then propels the boat across the water sideways. If the winds are moderate, you may be able to stand to cast. This adds to the wind resistance of the craft and increases the speed of the downwind drift. You can even control the speed and direction by having one or both fishermen in a boat stand, as their profiles act like a crude set

Casting long, multiple-fly leaders is easiest in open spaces or on lakes where there is room for backcasts.

of sails. Occasionally anchors are used to slow drifts. Because wind is critical to the drift, fishermen on these waters regard calm days with great scorn.

Lake boat fishermen use long rods, up to 15 feet, with a floating line, for reasons similar to those with river drift boats and to cast arrays of up to four flies. Anything more than a single backcast would result in hopelessly tangled leaders, and you make the cast with your back to the wind. The length of the rod compensates for the elimination of multiple false casts and allows the leader and two to four tippets to unfurl. Simple shooting casts may exceed 70 feet if you properly execute the technique. The formation of **S** curves is not critical in this type of fishing.

The long-rod casting techniques used in Ireland work best when the line and leader straighten out before they descend to the water surface. A moderate to strong wind aids in this regard and may even suspend the line and leader, allowing a very gentle presentation. The angler only briefly leaves the line still on the surface, as he must immediately retrieve line to prevent the boat from overtaking it in its drift. There is less concern for this when fishing from a drift boat on a stream, because both the water and the boat are moving, so the line moves downstream with both. In the case of lake drift fishing, however, the water is relatively current free, but the boat and fisherman are moving. So it is the exact converse of fishing from a stationary position on a stream. The retrieve may be varied, depending on the types of flies used and the experiences of fishermen on the particular lake. Take the advice of a trusted local fisherman when trying new water.

Although these are referred to as wet-fly techniques, dry flies or wet-fly patterns fished at the surface will also produce results. Some fishermen use an array consisting of a dry fly as the first fly, a wet fly representing an emerger or drowned adult as a middle fly, and a nymph as the point, or end, fly. The dry fly may be a pattern representative of a natural, or it may be an attractor used to get the fish to look in the general area, after which they may select either the wet fly or the nymph.

Depending on the size of the lake and the number of boats, several traverses, or drift lines may be covered, giving access to all areas assumed to hold fish. It is important to minimize motor travel through areas where you or someone else will be fishing that day, as the noise and commotion of a motor will put fish down for hours.

This type of fishing can be relaxing and casual if conditions are fair, but it can be exhilarating, even dangerous, if high winds or severe weather occurs. If there is lightning, keep in mind the high electrical conductivity of graphite rods and the great length of these rods.

GLOSSARY

Bobber—An object attached to fishing line to detect strikes or interruptions in natural drift. A plastic or foam float, a wad or tuft of floating yarn, or a bead of floating material can serve as a bobber.

Boulder—A detached rock of ten inches or greater.

Braided leaders—Leaders made from multiple strands woven together laterally (side-to-side) or in tubular fashion to form a single composite strand.

Buoyancy—The physical property that allows an object to float on water or some other fluid by virtue of its having a specific gravity less than that of the fluid.

Butt section—In a leader, the largest-diameter and generally the stiffest portion of the leader attached directly to the fly line. It may be a single segment or a compound tapered section. (See also *energy transfer section*.)

Cane rods—Fishing rods made from thin strips of bamboo that are assembled edge-to-edge in a ring, held together by adhesives, wraps of fine thread, or both.

Cast—The act of propelling the fly line, leader, and fly to their target. In Europe, a leader is also referred to as a cast.

Cobble—A detached rock greater than $2\frac{1}{2}$ inches and less than 10 inches in diameter.

Concave—Curved in an inward direction, as the inside of the letter C.

Convex—Curved in an outward direction, as the outside of the letter C is convex.

Current lanes—Continuous portions of a stream flowing at the same relative speed and direction, bounded on either side by the bank or obstructions, or similar lanes of current flowing at contrasting rates.

Current tubes—Current lanes that are bounded on all sides, including above and below (by the stream bottom, obstructions, air, or other current tubes with contrasting flow rates).

Double taper—Fly line with a taper that is symmetrical in both directions from the thickest point at the midpoint, so that the ends are finer in diameter than the middle section.

Drag—Resistance to unencumbered drift, as on a fly drifting in the current, imposed by the contrary movement or inertia of the fly line and leader. Also, a reel's friction-based braking system, which allows line to be pulled out under resistance.

Drift—In fly fishing, the course or route of the line, leader, and fly in or on the water.

Dropper—The segment of tippet for additional flies, attached at either the hook eye or bend, when more than one fly is used on a leader.

Ductile—The ability of a material to be permanently deformed without rupture. Ductile deformation occurs when a material is bent or flexed and remains in that form when at rest (without support); the deformation may occur with a change in volume due to compression or expansion.

Elastic—The ability of a material to be deformed without permanence. The deformation of elastic materials is recoverable; if the stress that causes deformation is removed, the object will return to its initial form.

Emerger—Transitional phase of an insect between nymph or pupa and winged stage. Emergers are more often fly patterns that are intended to represent this transition with body elements of both nymph/pupa and winged insect.

Energy-transfer section—The portion of the leader responsible for transferring the energy (loop) of the cast beyond the line to the leader so that the fly is propelled far enough from the line to achieve a proper presentation. (See also *butt section*.)

Fiberglass—A composite material consisting of fine glass fibers in a resin. Tubular fiberglass fly rods became popular in the 1950s and were replaced by graphite composite rods in the 1980s.

Flexibility—The ability to bend without breaking or rupture.

Float—To remain atop the water surface through either buoyancy or surface tension. Also, an object used to float a section of line or act as a strike or drag indicator.

Floatant—A material applied to line to aid in keeping it afloat due to surface tension.

Fluorocarbon—A polymer compound containing fluorine and carbon, used in fly fishing as a leader material. Fluorocarbon has a specific gravity greater than water and is more flexible than nylon. It does not degrade in ultraviolet light, its optical properties render it less visible in water than nylon, and it is impervious to water. Its breaking strength is less than nylon of equivalent diameter. Because of its molecular structure, it has a lower coefficient of friction and requires additional care in knotting.

Furled leaders—Leaders made by twining or twisting multiple fibers or strands into a single strand, held together like rope or twine by the torsion of individual strands.

Graphite—A rigid pure carbon material used in composite with resin base for high-strength applications, including fly rods.

Gut—Tough cord derived from the digestive tract of an animal, often used for leaders, tennis rackets, and musical instruments.

Laminar flow—Flow of a fluid, such as water, in an uninterrupted or unimpeded path without lateral deviation from the primary flow direction.

Leader—A length of line between the fly and the permanent fly line. It performs several functions, including separating the fly from the more visible fly line and presenting the fly to the fish in a more natural drift.

Line slap—The impact of line or leader hitting the surface of the water, causing shock waves that can startle or spook fish.

Load—The transfer of kinetic energy of the cast (energy of the arm's movement) to potential energy in the flexed fly rod. The greater the loading, the deeper the rod will bend.

Mend—Manipulation of the fly line, usually after the fly has landed on the water, to counter the effects of drag by adding slack line or flipping the line upstream or down to obtain the desired action. Mending is done to correct the position of the line with respect to currents and the preferred presentation, either immediately following the forward cast or as the fly drifts and correction is required.

Modulus of elasticity—The physical parameter that measures the extent to which a body or material will deform (strain) in response to stress. A material with a low modulus of elasticity is more readily deformable than one with a higher modulus. Also known as Young's modulus.

Momentum—The product of mass times velocity. According to the laws of physics, in the absence of friction and gravity, angular momentum is conserved. So if energy is transferred from one object to another, the product of these (mass times velocity) will be equal before and after the transfer. Thus, if a heavy fly line is moving at a rate of 3 feet per second, and this energy is transmitted to a leader that is half the mass of the fly line, the leader will move at 6 feet per second if no other forces act on the line and leader.

Monofilament—Line consisting of a continuous single, thin fiber.

Node—Upper or lower points in the sinuous waveform corresponding to crests and troughs in a wave.

Nylon—Synthetic thermoplastics with great strength and elasticity, often used for line and leaders.

Nymph—Nonflying or larval stage of aquatic insects that typically forage on microscopic plant and animal materials. In fly fishing, the term is sometimes used to describe nearly any subsurface pattern without wings.

Plastic—Capable of being permanently deformed without breaking, usually accompanied by a change in volume of the material. Also, a synthetic organic compound capable of being shaped under pressure or heat.

Plasticizer—Any compound added to plastic compounds to increase flexibility.

Point fly—The fly tied to the end of the last tippet segment when more than one fly is used.

Polymer—A generally plastic compound formed by combinations of repeating carbon-based compounds in long sequences.

Polyurethane—Synthetic soft polymers formed by combining isocyanate with hydroxide compounds. Produced as resins, thermoplastics, or foams.

Polyvinyl chloride (PVC)—A polymer that when treated with plasticizers is used as the outer coating of most fly lines. PVC is not resistant to ultraviolet light and will become brittle in time if exposed to sunlight or excessive heat.

Presentation section—The portion of the leader closest to the fly, responsible for allowing the fly to attain the desired presentation or drift. The presentation section generally consists of one to three segments of thinner, more supple material, longer than the transition taper.

Refractive index—The ratio of the velocity of light passing through a vacuum (c) to its velocity in a medium (v): Refractive index = c/v

Resin—Any of a class of natural or synthetic compounds that occur in a semisolid form, similar to rosin or sap, and become plastic under certain conditions.

Rupture—Nonrecoverable deformation of material; breakage.

Specific gravity—A comparison of material mass per unit volume with that of pure water. Water is assumed to have a specific gravity of 1.0. Materials with a specific gravity less than 1.0 will float (be buoyant) in water, those with a specific gravity greater than 1.0 will sink in water once submerged below the surface.

Strike indicator—A floating device attached to the leader or line to provide a high-visibility indication of a strike. (See also *bobber.*)

Strip—To retrieve line following a cast. The rate of retrieve varies with the desired purpose—to simulate a specific natural behavior, to stimulate a strike, or to simply retrieve the line before the next cast.

Stripping guide—The large line guide on a fly rod, located closest to the reel. The stripping guide is larger in diameter to facilitate efficient shooting of fly line in the cast and often has an inner ring of a low-friction material to help shooting line.

Surface tension—The resistance to puncture or breach of the surface of a fluid by a solid object. The tendency of water particles to adhere to themselves rather than the contrasting solid maintains a barrier to penetration, keeping the solid afloat. When the weight of the solid exceeds the strength of the bond between water particles, the object may sink if not buoyant. Materials having high surface tension with respect to water will float even if they have a greater specific gravity than water.

Suspended load—Buoyant and nonbuoyant material transported by a stream, kept from settling on the bottom by virtue of stream turbulence, relative density, and object shape.

Taper—Continuous (knotless) or compound (tied) material that is thicker at one end than the other.

Tippet—Thinner-diameter material used in the presentation section of a leader. Tippet sometimes refers to the last segment of the leader to which the fly is tied.

Transition taper—The portion of the leader that tapers from the stiffer energy-transfer section to the thinner presentation section. Generally composed of shorter segments of decreasing diameter.

Turbidity—A reduction of clarity of water caused by dissolved and suspended material.

Turbulence—Irregular flow of a fluid, resulting in nonlinear flow patterns.

Viscoelastic—Flowing deformation of otherwise solid material under pressure, which may or may not be recoverable and occurs with a change in relative volume.

Weight-forward—A fly line with a taper that is asymmetrical, having a more gradual front (toward the leader) section and a steeper back section, with a long, nontapered, thinner "running line" section between the base of the forward taper and the reel. Marketed under various names, including rocket taper, torpedo taper, and bass bug taper.

REFERENCES

Ball, John. *Casting and Fishing the Artificial Fly.* Caldwell, ID: Caxton Printers, 1972.

Beegle, Bernard. "Convex Tapered Leaders." *Fly Fisherman* 14, no. 6 (September 1983).

Bergman, Ray. *Trout.* Lanham, MD: New York: Penn Press, 1938. (Derrydale Press, 2000.)

Black, William. *Creekcraft.* Boulder, CO: Pruett Publishing Co., 1988.

———. *Flyfishing the Rockies.* Boulder, CO: Pruett Publishing Co., 1976.

Borger, Gary. *Presentation.* Wausau, WI: Tomorrow River Press, 1996.

Borger, Jason. "The Bow and Arrow." *Fly Fish America* (May 1999).

Callsiter, William D., Jr. *Material Science and Engineering.* New York: John Wiley & Sons, 1994.

Caucci, Al. "The Krazy Glue Leader Splice." *Fly Fisherman* 17, no. 1 (December 1995): 50.

Clark, Peter, and Howard Croston. "The Mighty Midge." *Fly Fishing and Fly Tying* (July–August 1999): 4.

Clarke, Brian. *Pursuit of Stillwater Trout.* London: A. C. Black, 1975.

Engerbretsen, Dave. *Leader Design and Construction.* www.finefishing.com/flyfish/equipment/leaderdesign.htm.

Fahey, Douglas. *A Concise History of Plastics.* New South Wales Plastics Manufacturing Training Body, Ltd., home page: www.nswpmitb.com.au. (September 1999).

Fujimoto, Takatoshi. Personal communication, October 27, 2000. Sunline Company, Yamaguchi, Japan.

Goddard, John. *Trout Fishing Techniques.* New York: Lyons & Burford, 1996.

Goddard, John, and Brian Clark. *The Trout and the Fly.* London: A. C. Black, 1980.

Gowans, Alistair. "Underhand Questions." *Fly Fishing and Fly Tying* (May 2001): 74–76.

Harvey, George. *Techniques for Fly Fishing.* New York: Lyons & Burford, 1990.

———. "Harvey's New Leader Formula." *Fly Fisherman* 32 no. 6 (September 2001): 38–39.

———. Personal Communication, July 12, 2001.

Hoffmann, J. A., and M. R. Hooper. "Fly Rod Response." *Journal of Sound and Vibration* 209, no. 3 (1998): 537–41.

Hoffmann, Jon A., Matthew R. Hooper, and Al Kyte. *Rod Stiffness and Line Weight Rating.* Unpublished. June 1999.

Hoffmann, Jon A., and Prov Reth. "The Motion of a Fly Line. Part A: Governing Equations." Proceedings of DETC '99, 1999 ASME Design Engineering Technical Conferences, September 12–15, 1999, Las Vegas, Nevada.

———. "The Motion of a Fly Line. Part B: Solutions." Proceedings of DETC '99, 1999 ASME Design Engineering Technical Conferences, September 12–15, 1999, Las Vegas, Nevada.

Humphreys, Joe. *Trout Tactics.* Mechanicsburg, PA: Stackpole, 1992.

Judy, John. *Slack Line Strategies for Fly Fishing.* Mechanicsburg, PA: Stackpole, 1994.

Klausmeyer, David. "Tying Your Own Nymphs." *Fly Fisherman* 26, no. 5 (July 1995): 62–65.

Kreh, Lefty. *Advanced Techniques for Fly Fishing.* New York: Dell, 1992.

———. *Fly Fishing in Salt Water.* New York: Lyons & Burford, 1986.

———. *Longer Fly Casting.* New York: Lyons & Burford, 1990.

———. *Presenting the Fly.* New York: Lyons Press, 1999.

LaFontaine, Gary. *Caddisflies.* New York: Lyons & Burford, 1981.

Lee, Art. *Tying and Fishing the Riffling Hitch.* Champaign, IL: Human Kinetics, 1998.

Martin, Darrel. *Micropatterns.* New York: Lyons & Burford, 1994.

Matthews, Craig. *Western Fly Fishing Strategies.* New York: Lyons Press, 1998.

McDaniel, John. "The Delicate Nymph." *Fly Fisherman* 27, no. 4 (March 1996): 72–80.

McGuire, John, Ph.D. "Notes on Semi-Rigid Connections." NASA Goddard Space Flight Center. http://analyst.gsfc.nasa.gov/FEMCI/SemiRigid/. (1995).

Merwin, John. *The New American Trout Fishing.* New York: Macmillan Publishing Co., 1994.

Meyer, Deke. "Right Angle Nymphing Leader." *Fly Fisherman* 24, no. 2 (February 1993): 58.

Notley, Larry. *Fly Leaders and Knots.* Portland, OR: Frank Amato, 1996.

Orvis Company. Personal communication with technical advisor Jeremy Benn, February 17, 1999.

Passante, Jeff. "2-Fly Rigs." *Fly Fisherman* 29, no. 3 (March 1998): 78.

Phillips, Don. "Another Dimension for Fly Rod Evaluation . . . Stiffness Profile." *Fly Fisherman* 4, no. 6 (June–July 1973).

————. *The Technology of Fly Rods.* Portland, OR: Frank Amato Books, 1999.

Price, Taff. *Tying and Fishing the Nymph.* London: Blandford, 1995.

Richards, Carl. *Prey.* New York: Lyons & Burford, 1995.

Ritz, Charles. *A Fly Fisher's Life.* New York: Henry Holt, 1959.

Rosenbauer, Tom. *Leaders, Knots and Tippets.* New York: Lyons Press, 2000.

————. *Prospecting for Trout.* New York: Dell, 1993.

————. *Reading Trout Streams.* New York: Lyons Press, 1988.

Spolek, G.A. "Fly Rod Action Quantified." *Fly Fisherman* 25, no. 1 (December 1993): 42–45.

Sternberg, Dick, David Tieszen, and John van Vliet. *Fly Fishing for Trout in Streams: Subsurface Techniques.* Minneapolis: Cowles, 1996.

Taylor, Bernie. "Testing Knots." *Fly Fisherman* 27, no. 1 (December 1995): 52.

Teeny, Jim. *Steelhead and Salmon.* Birmingham, AL: Odysseus Editions, 1996.

Walton, Isaak, and James Cotton. (Raines ed.) *The Compleat Angler.* New York: Random House, 1996.

Whitlock, Dave. *Fly Fishing for Bass Handbook.* New York: Lyons & Burford, 1988.

————. *Guide to Aquatic Trout Foods and Their Imitation.* New York: Nick Lyons Books, 1982.

Wright, Leonard. *Trout Maverick.* New York: Lyons & Burford, 1996.

Wulff, Lee. *Atlantic Salmon.* New York: A. S. Barnes & Co., 1958.

————. *Trout on a Fly.* New York: Lyons Press, 1986.

Yeomans, Steve. "Casting without a Fly Line." *Fly Fishing and Fly Tying* (June 1999).

INDEX

Our editors recommend . . .

TROUBLESHOOTING
THE CAST

by Ed Jaworowski
illustrated by Harry W. Robertson III

Expert diagnoses and solutions for
32 fly-casting problems.

$12.95 • PB • 96 pages • 120 line drawings

WWW.STACKPOLEBOOKS.COM
1–800–732–3669